# Creative
# Hamburger Cookery

## 182 Unusual Recipes for Casseroles
## Meat Loaves and Hamburgers

by

### LOUIS P. De GOUY

DOVER PUBLICATIONS, INC.
NEW YORK

Published in Canada by General Publishing Company, Ltd., 30 Lesmill Road, Don Mills, Toronto,
Ontario.
Published in the United Kingdom by Constable
and Company, Ltd., 10 Orange Street, London WC 2.


This Dover edition, first published in 1974, is an
unabridged republication of the work originally
published in 1951 by Greenberg Publisher under the
title *The Burger Book*.


*International Standard Book Number: 0-486-23001-5*
*Library of Congress Catalog Card Number: 73-88330*

Manufactured in the United States of America
Dover Publications, Inc.
180 Varick Street
New York, N. Y. 10014

# THE AUTHOR'S INTRODUCTION

A friend in need; a guide to your own observation, good judgment, and memory; a hoard of valuable suggestions to aid you in time of doubt—that is what you may expect of any good cookbook, and it is a great deal.

With all the excellent markets, where all kinds of raw materials and the ever-growing number of prepared foods are delivered fresh daily, the modern homemaker does not have to spend much time to plan her meals. With the convenience of the telephone, groceries and meat may be had at short notice, and meals need be planned only from day to day. These conditions are in favor of the modern cook, whether she cooks on the latest gas or electric stove or totes her fuel from the woodpile, which still is done on many farms in this great country of ours, to the surprise of many city dwellers. These and many more conveniences are things that great-grandmother—and even just grandmother—never dared to dream of.

But that is where the magic of this age stops! For markets, conveniences, and books galore on cooking will never set a good meal on the table without the skill and devotion of a really good cook. Regulating the oven temperature is very important. Is the heat evenly distributed? Many a cake, pie, or custard has been ruined with too much heat in the back and not enough in front and on the sides. Knowing the time when a pie has reached that golden hue—for one precious minute or two more may turn it burned and uneatable—and the basting of a roast so that it will not taste dry are details that only diligent practice and experience can teach the novice. She must learn such things herself, no matter how many cookbooks she reads, or how much time she spends in going to food shows and watching expert demonstrations. Once these are accomplished, the new cook can serve good, balanced, and healthful meals for family and guests.

Here are a few general rules that should lighten the work in planning one dish or a whole menu. To begin with, if you are not sure of the selected recipe, or do not know it by heart, place your friend, the cookbook, open flat on the table—and keep it open. Read the recipe through once—even twice—if necessary, to get all the things you will need firmly established in your mind. Next,

iii

select all the utensils and ingredients, and place them within easy reach.

Proceed to think out, one by one in their correct order, the various steps of measuring, mixing, heating or melting, beating, basting, and so on, whatever the recipe calls for. See that the flame is right, or that the oven is at the right temperature, exactly as you want it. In short, overlook nothing that will save you time and prevent unfortunate—and expensive—mistakes. Then, if your luck is poor, it will not be due to carelessness.

Be not deceived by the apparent nonchalance with which an expert cook or master chef throws together an attractive and tempting meal. It is merely proof that, through practical experience, she or he knows thoroughly all the steps and preparation that seem to follow each other so automatically to a successful conclusion. No beginner should feel ashamed to depend on whatever help other people can give, either through printed recipes or by personal instruction.

Remember that a recipe is the fruit of practical experience. Someone experimented some time long ago, perhaps failed at first, tried again and again, finally succeeded, and passed on the result by word of mouth to others. There were good cooks long before there were printed or written recipes. Some recipes, however, have been handed down from Roman times, and recipes have been printed as early as the sixteenth century. Modern recipes are more accurate than the old, as may be seen if one has the opportunity to read some old cookbooks.

Therefore, if it is the first time you are attempting to use a certain recipe, *follow its directions exactly!* This never can be stressed enough. Notice the proportions, and use the specified amounts (which nowadays is such a pleasant task with easily read quantity markings on cups and spoons). Read carefully the directions for combining the ingredients, and follow them, noticing the points that are most important. Have the entire operation well in mind before you even attempt to begin working with the ingredients. By completely understanding all the steps before you start, you will not need to refer to the printed instructions at every move, which is really poor technique.

When you are no longer a beginner, a few liberties may be taken in the preparation of a recipe, even a new one, by looking it over with a critical eye to see where a variation may be substituted. Perhaps you remember that old saying from schooldays, "Necessity is the mother of invention." With that in mind, if you are short of one or two ingredients, you may substitute something else if it combines properly with the rest of the mixture.

Do not take a recipe formula too seriously. It may not be entirely a new one. For this is the secret of recipes: there are really only a few absolutely original formulas, although they wear all varieties of decoration and garb. Study and learn the "tricks of the trade," and then with practical experience, you too will become inventive and can make your own variations.

Did you know that the word "recipe" is from the Latin word meaning "take"? Follow this advice and "take" or bring together on the worktable whatever material you need. As you gather the ingredients, take, measure, and weigh the exact amounts as directed.

The preparation and assembly of a number of dishes for a meal calls for a skill, a practical ability considerably different from that needed for the making of just one single dish. Whatever the menu decided on, it must be, above all, a well-balanced meal in nutrition; second, it should have an attractive color scheme. All this needs forethought, an accurate sense of time, imagination, and promptness, to assemble a number of dishes and have them ready at the same time, or in proper sequence if several courses are served.

The fact is obvious that, in the preparation of a meal, each dish cannot be finished one at a time, so to speak, but steps individual to each dish must be interwoven with others. All the courses of the meal must be on the mind of the homemaker, who must attend to a dozen or more things at one time.

THIS BOOK IS FONDLY DEDICATED

TO THE MEMORY OF

# LOUIS P. DE GOUY
## (1876-1947)

BY HIS DAUGHTER

JACQUELINE S. DOONER

# Contents

Page

Part One   **BEEF BURGERS**       1

Tips for Using Herbs and Spices—Original Hamburg Steak As Made in Hamburg, Germany—Burger Balls—En Brochette—Beef Burger Essence and Extract—Casseroles—Chop Suey—Collops—Croquettes—Custards—Cutlets—Dinners—Dumplings—Fricadelles—Fricassee—Au Gratin—Griddle Cakes—Grills—Individual Loaves—Luncheons—Omelets — Pasties — Patties — Pies — Puddings — Rarebit — Rings — Rolls — Sausages — Shortcake — Soufflés—Soup—Steaks—Stews—Timbales—Turnovers—Waffles

Part Two   **BURGER LOAVES**      91

Burger Loaves—with Cheese—Fruit—Macaroni—Sour Cream—Vegetables—Wine—Including Layer —Pinwheel—Ribbon—Ring Forms

"The sharing of a favorite recipe is a bond which brings us all a little closer together." And as Master Escoffier once said: "In cooking there is always something new to try. Times change and seasons change, today you are rich and tomorrow you are poor, and cooking must fit itself to all that comes. No cook who knows a little about cooking, and interests himself or herself in it, should ever find it dull."

The cook must be precise in her calculations, must know not only how to prepare food, but also the whys and wherefores, the nature of the material she employs, the necessity for it, the quantity required, the time of cooking, the weight of the different ingredients used, and the meaning of them. The cook, man or woman, must be an artist in the complicated, delicate, and responsible art of cookery.

LOUIS P. DE GOUY

# PART ONE

# *Beef Burgers*

Tips for Using Herbs and Spices—Original Hamburg Steak As Made in Hamburg, Germany—Burger Balls—En Brochette—Beef Burger Essence and Extract—Casseroles—Chop Suey—Collops—Croquettes — Custards — Cutlets — Dinners — Dumplings — Frica-delles—Fricassee—Au Gratin—Griddle Cakes—Grills—Individual Loaves—Luncheons—Omelets—Pasties—Patties—Pies—Puddings—Rarebit—Rings—Rolls—Sausages—Shortcake—Soufflés—Soup—Steaks—Stews—Timbales—Turnovers—Waffles

## MEAT ON THE TABLE

I sing this glorious land of ours,
  Its motor cars and shows,
Its little gardens, gay with flowers,
  Its phones and radios.
Here your ambitious boy may be
  Our President if he's able,
But what spells U.S.A. to me
  Is "meat upon the table!"

Ours is the land of steaks and chops,
  Of pork, beef, lamb and veal,
And thrifty costs when woman shops
  Put meat in any meal.
So if at us should any scoff
  Just show this patriot label—
One reason we are better off
  Is "meat upon the table."

EDGAR A. GUEST

# BEEF BURGERS

It's not the cooking of three meals a day that gets a woman down, it's the planning—trying to find something everybody likes, something a little different, something that fits into the food budget easily. That's why hamburger, be it in pat-a-cake, ring, or loaf form, is so popular for menus. You can do many things with it, dress it up in any number of ways with sauces and stuffings. It's a favorite with the menfolk, easy to prepare, and economical. It does not take much cooking, and is a god-send on busy days, summer days, and winter days. With burger for a starter, you can make a meal that is substantial enough for the family or guest dinner, and economical enough for a company spread.

When you want to save money and still want some really tasty meat for dinner, what do you think of? Why burgers of course. It's not the meat alone, it's what you put with it that counts.

Hamburgers are stylish, popular, and proper. With mustard, tomato catsup, or cheese, they go into the upper brackets. It takes something more than just a hot-dog stand to make a burger. Burgers cooked to perfection are a real culinary art.

Burgers can be not only a fine nourishing food, but a varied food, and being also inexpensive, the wise cook and homemaker may feel justified in allowing herself a few frills now and then, so that meat balls will have neither the taste nor the appearance of poverty. Do not be misled by our calling burgers inexpensive. In this case, we mean that it is economical on the pocketbook, not that you are skimping on the health of your family when serving any one of the varied recipes in this cookbook.

An extra dab of butter, a dash of this and of that, slowly mixing and blending with the pink juices of the well-browned meat or a few mushrooms for a sauce, for variety's sake, are all economies in the long run, since not only is it a saving on the food budget, but it heightens as well as preserves the family appetite for burgers in-definitely.

There are important do's and don'ts that make the difference between a mediocre and superior burger. Beware of buying bargain-price burger meat at any time, at any place. It is usually from the less desirable cuts, and may be excessively fat, so that it shrinks badly in cooking.

For ground veal and lamb, buy shoulder or breast cuts, rather than the more costly leg.

The favorite and most economical beef cuts that are chopped or ground for burgers are round, chuck, neck, lower round, plate, and flank. Buy chuck or plate beef for grinding, whether for patties or loaf. Both round and flank steaks are too lean to make juicy burger, and in this cookbook are suggested only for certain types of recipes. The chuck and plate cuts are more economical in price. Buy your favorite cut, but be sure that there is at least 15 per cent fat content to insure uniformity of flavor. Have it ground not too fine. This applies also to burger loaves.

The trouble with most kitchen economies is that they are undertaken with an eye only on the budget, whereas the imaginative cook keeps one eye on the budget and the other cocked critically on the quality and variety of her menus. It is only by this kind of coordination that kitchen economies can be made painless.

There are two ways of bringing down food costs—there may be a great many more as practiced by the stern breed of Puritans who only eat to live—but these remarks are addressed to charming people who like to eat well. The really successful cook and budgeteer knows that she can arrive at the same result by one of two ways. Either she can take a coarse and cheap food, and spend a few extra cents (as well as more care) on its accompaniments, or serve a slightly more expensive food, which is fine enough in itself to stand a lowly accompaniment.

It is a pity that burgers have got a bad name with some people because of dull cooks who, when faced with a serious bout of household economy, cannot think of a blessed thing but chopped beef. And no harm in that either, except that such cooks can find nothing to do with a burger but fry it—and that not any too well.

Fortunately, many people feel about hamburgers much as did the young lad who returned from a coast-to-coast automobile trip and boasted that he had eaten them in every stopping place from the Atlantic to the Pacific.

Hamburgers essentially are patties made of ground beef, but many parts of the country have different ways of preparing them. The names under which burgers are served are as various as the

methods of making them—meat balls, meat cakes, hamburger croquettes, chopped beef patties are but a few.

The origin of hamburgers is lost in the annals of cookery, but
the original recipe came from Hamburg, Germany (see No. 1),
where the dish is quite different from those served in America. As
you study this cookbook, you will see that there is a lot of difference in these hamburger recipes.

The right herbs and spices for the various ingredients help to
make ground beef and other meats interesting and exceedingly
flavorful. So that you will understand what each suggested herb is
expected to do to the ingredients of these recipes, a table of how
and when to use herbs and spices in meats and other foods follows.


## COOKING WITH HERBS AND SPICES

It's fun to cook with herbs and spices! These neglected seasonings too often take a back seat on the pantry shelf, while the cook
relies solely on salt and pepper to pep up chops, stews, sauces,
gravies, and the popular hamburger family. Meals are apt to reach
a low ebb if the food always tastes the same. Grandmother solved
this problem by using herbs and spices from the garden to heighten
the flavor of everyday dishes. Successful she was, and successful
you'll be, if you learn to cook with them.

If there is anything that makes family and guests take special
interest in a menu, it is the cook's ability to serve a dish that is
outstanding in its marked fine flavor. When seasoning food, do not
overlook the many beloved old herbs too often forgotten in hasty
cooking. These seasonings give a certain individuality and goodness to dishes that otherwise might have little flavor.

The use of spices in cooking is like make-up on a woman. They
should be so deftly added that they add glamor, and so skillfully
blended that they are not obvious. Then they achieve an artistic
elusiveness that captivates the senses. There are three ways to in-
troduce herbs and spices as seasoning for foods: (1) add the herb
or spice as seasoning while cooking the food; (2) mince the green
herbs and sprinkle over the food before serving; or (3) use the
essence of the herb or spice.

Synthetic spices, including cinnamon, mace, nutmeg, and ginger,
are commercial developments designed to meet the shortage of

imported spices. These synthetic spices have general characteristics, taste, and aroma similar to those of the corresponding natural spices, and they cost much less, and may be purchased in any quantity.

If spices are kept tightly covered, even to the sifter cap, they will retain their full body and strength for months. But any spice that has been exposed to the air for a period of time, or has stood for more than a year in the kitchen closet, is bound to have lost most of its value as a seasoner. The delicate oils that give spices their appetizing smell and hunger-stirring taste when mixed with other ingredients must be protected from the air to preserve them intact.

## TIPS FOR USING HERBS AND SPICES

1. Spices and herbs should be blended with food in cooking and before serving, not served with the food.

2. Use sparingly. Aromatic oils are strong, and too much of any flavor is unpleasant.

3. A scant ¼ teaspoon of dry herbs or spices for every 4 servings seasons food best.

4. Chop fresh herbs, and crumble dried herbs, finely before using, for fullest flavor.

5. To avoid monotony, limit the use of highly flavored seasonings to two in any one meal.

6. To prevent mistakes, remember that dried herbs are 4 times as strong as fresh herbs.

7. The flavor of herbs is lost if the cooking time is long. Add them during the last hour of cooking.

8. To season cold salads or beverages, let spices and herbs stand in the food for several hours.

Here is a table to help you choose the right seasoning for the right food. Pay heed to the hints above, then settle down for an adventure in good eating.

| NAME | FLAVOR | USE IN COOKING |
|---|---|---|
| Alder (black) | Like tea | Also called Appalachian tea and evergreen winterberry; used for tea |

| | | |
|---|---|---|
| Allspice | Strong clove and cinnamon | Soups, sauces, fish, meats, vegetables, pickling, flavorings; tasty in cakes, cookies, bread; Carolina allspice used in synthetic cinnamon |
| Anise<br>Anise seeds | Strong licorice | In breads, cakes, cookies, candy, tea, cordials, liquors |
| Arnato or butter coloring | No flavor | For coloring butter, cheese, inferior chocolates; harmless in foods |
| Bay leaf | Mild, dry, or semifresh; aromatic | Improves stews, soups, pickling, preserving, marinating, sauces, gumbo, boiled fish |
| Borage | Taste of oysters; aromatic; young leaves smell like cucumber | In beverages, salads; boiled like spinach; a spike adds allure to tomato juice cocktail |
| Burnet | Smells like cucumber | To flavor greens, salads; in beverages |
| Capers | Taste like gherkins | Seasoning fish, meats, game, soups, sauces, salads, preserves; as garnish for cold cuts and fish when mixed with mayonnaise and pickles |
| Caraway seeds | Warm, pungent, aromatic | In cakes, cookies; in soups, sauerkraut, cream or cottage cheese; in coffee, tea, other beverages |
| Cardamom seeds | Mild, sweet, aromatic, subtle | In pastries, cookies, cakes, coffee; also chewing gum, candies, breads |

| Celery seeds | Celery flavor, but mild | In pickles, relishes, catsup, soups, sauces, stews, sauerkraut |
| --- | --- | --- |
| Chervil | Aromatic like parsley, but milder; root flavor when boiled intermediate between that of chestnut and potato | Same uses as parsley |
| **Chili** | Fiery, pungent | In soups, sauces, stews, fish, pickling; whole in tamale and rice |
| Chives | Mild onion flavor | In soups, sandwiches, omelets, salads, potatoes, meats, sausages |
| Cinnamon | Sweet, warm, aromatic | In beverages, desserts, soups, fish, meats, poultries, game, pastries, cordials, liquors, baked products, preserves, oil extract, pancakes, waffles, sauces |
| Cloves | Strong, warm, aromatic, pungent | Seasoning soups, sauces, beverages, stews, stuffings, baked products, pickles, oil extract, liquors, cordials; combines with cinnamon in meats and baked products; tasty in chocolate pudding and hot beverages |
| Coriander | Quite aromatic | In sausages, baked products, candies, cordials, pastries, gingerbread, pickling, coffee |

| | | |
|---|---|---|
| Cumin or comino | Stimulating, aromatic, pungent | In cordials and liquors, curry powder, sauerkraut, cabbage, potatoes, baked goods |
| Curry powder—a mixture of more than sixteen spices and condiments | Hot, pungent, stimulating; cooling and heating at the same time | Pinch adds zip to soups, gravies, sauces, fish, meats, poultry, vegetables, preserving |
| Dill | Aromatic, stimulating | In pickling, sausages, sauerkraut, cucumbers, cabbage; in making vinegar; to season meats, furred game |
| Fennel or finocchio | Aromatic, licorice | Bulb stewed; stalks served as celery; in vegetables, certain Italian meat, fish, poultry dishes |
| Garlic | Strong-scented, pungent, astringent | Small slice or clove adds pep and flavor to meat, fish, poultry, game, casserole dishes, salads, stuffings, salad dressing |
| Ginger | Fiery when used in large quantity; pungent, aromatic | Adds snappy taste to cakes, cookies, numerous desserts, relishes, pickling, curries |
| Horehound | Bitter | Candies, confections, liquors, cordials |
| Horseradish | Pungent | Sauces, salads, pickles; adulterant is white turnip |
| Hyssop | Mint, spicy, bitter, hot | In soups, salads, greens, fruits, beverages, candies |

| | | |
|---|---|---|
| Irish moss | No flavor | Substitute for gelatin in desserts for children, invalids |
| Juniper berries | Aromatic | In sauces and stuffing for game |
| Lemon balm | Aromatic | In soups, sauces, desserts |
| Licorice | Aromatic | In candies, confections, syrups, cordials |
| Mace | Fragrant, mild; nutmeg flavor | Gives distinct flavor to cakes, cookies, puddings, baked products; in sauces, stuffings, sausages |
| Marjoram | Mild, sweet, aromatic | Excellent mixer with other herbs; blends well with meats, poultry, vegetables |
| Mint | Fragrant odor and pleasant taste | In sauces for lamb, mutton; in confections, beverages |
| Mustard | Sharp, peppery, pungent | Seasoning for sauces, fish, meats, poultry, game, salads, pickles, condiments, cold cuts, delicatessen products |
| Nutmeg | Nutty, trace of pepper | Excellent mixer with cloves and cinnamon in seasoning fish, meats, poultry, game, stuffings, baked products, confections, desserts, puddings, cordials, liquors |
| Oregano | Same as thyme, but milder | Same uses as thyme |

| | | |
|---|---|---|
| Paprika | Sweet; slightly peppery | Adds nip to sauces, mayonnaise, salad dressings, stuffings |
| Parsley | Aromatic | Seasons almost any kind of food, except baked sweets, confections; most popular garnish |
| Pepper: black and white | Pungent | Peppercorn, though small, seasons every dish except sweet ones |
| Poppy seeds | Sweet, pungent, aromatic | To season and flavor cakes, cookies, pastries, bread, noodles, pastes, appetizers, pickles, condiments, preserves, beverages |
| Poultry seasoning | Blend of pepper, sage, marjoram, mace | Seasons almost any kind of food, except desserts, candies; greatly used in sausage |
| Rosemary | Sweet-sharp; fragrant, resinous taste | To flavor almost any kind of cooked meat, soups, preserves, sauces; garnish for green salads, rosemary wine, rosemary biscuits |
| Saffron | Mildly pungent, aromatic | In breads, pickles, bouillabaise, fish, meat, poultry, sauces; imparts yellow coloring to confections, cordials, liquors, rice, cabbage |
| Sage | Strong, pungent, mucilaginous | Fish, stews, stuffings, onions, pork dishes, sauces |

| | | |
|---|---|---|
| Salt | One of the most important raw material seasonings in the world; no flavor | Used in everything in the diet; very little, but essential; decreases sourness of acids and increases sweetness of sugars |
| Sassafras—from sassafras is made the Creole filé | Aromatic, spicy, stimulating | In homemade beer, Creole cookery, confections, beverages; adds piquancy to soups, fish, sauces, meat, game, egg dishes, vegetables |
| Savory | Minted; mild sage-lemon-pepper | Gives subtle lift to meat dishes, stuffings, salads, vegetable cocktails; some soups and veal dishes improved by a little |
| Sesame seeds | Aromatic, slightly pungent, stimulating, nutty | In cakes, cookies, breads, certain desserts |
| Shallots | Mild onion flavor | Used in any dish calling for onion, or in addition to it |
| Sweet basil | Mild pepper-lemon-clove, aromatic | Same uses as savory |
| Tabasco sauce | Hot, spicy, pungent | Substitute for chili pepper; to be used cautiously in seasoning soups, sauces, gravies, fish, meat, poultry, game, salads |
| Tansy, also called costmary or alecost | Aromatic | Greatly used in Europe to flavor sauces, green salads, poultry stuffings |

| Tarragon | Aromatic, soporific | For seasoning sauces, soups, meat stews, salads, stuffings, gravies |
| Thyme | Piny, pungent, aromatic. Has lemon, orange, and caraway-scented cousins | Most popular seasoning for soups, stews, stuffings, fish, meats, poultry, game, pickling |
| Turmeric | Aromatic, pungent, stimulating | To color and give an egg-yolk yellow hue to light-tinted foods, cakes, cookies, butter, cheese; greatly used in pickling, condiments, curry powder |
| Woodruff, also called waldmeister | Fragrant, aromatic | Greatly used in punch bowls, candies, confections |

(1)

## ORIGINAL HAMBURG STEAK AS MADE IN HAMBURG, GERMANY

Use thin uncooked slices of round beef. Pound them a little to tenderize the meat. Divide into portions the size of a demitasse saucer. On each portion, sprinkle a little thyme or savory, a little pepper, and a dusting of salt to taste. Over this seasoning, spread 1 tablespoon of chopped onions. Place a portion of veal kidney suet over each slice, on top of the chopped onion. Roll up and secure with string at both ends and in the center, or with little wooden skewers or toothpicks, to keep in shape. Roll in salted and peppered flour, and place in a frying pan, in which has been heated a little butter or bacon drippings. Brown all around, over a bright flame. Then carefully pour over enough water or meat stock to barely cover the meat rolls. Cover tightly, reduce to the lowest possible flame, and allow to simmer very gently, turning the meat rolls occasionally. A little more gravy may be made by browning some flour, after lifting out the rolls, and thinning it with boiling water or meat stock.

## APPLE AND BURGER PATTIES     (2)
*Serves 6 generously*

6 slices stale bread
6 large green apples, peeled, cored, and quartered
1 dozen sprigs parsley, stemmed
1 dozen sprigs chives
1 extra large onion, coarsely chopped
2 whole fresh eggs, slightly beaten
2 pounds ground beef

2 teaspoons salt, or more to taste
½ generous teaspoon thyme leaves
1 generous pinch black pepper to taste
1 blade each mace, summer savory, nutmeg, and coriander, all powdered
Fine bread crumbs

Combine the apples, bread, parsley, chives, and onions, and put through a food chopper, using the medium blade. Mix thoroughly with all the remaining ingredients, except the bread crumbs. Form into 6 oblong patties of equal size. Roll in fine bread crumbs. When ready to serve, pan-fry in hot fat until brown on all sides. Serve with your favorite tomato, mushroom, or brown sauce.

## ARIZONA CHILI BURGERS     (3)
*Serves 6*

2 pounds ground fresh beef
2 medium-sized onions, chopped
1 tablespoon parsley, chopped
1 tablespoon chives, chopped
¾ scant teaspoon salt
No pepper
1 clove garlic, chopped fine
1 blade each thyme, mace, and marjoram

¼ cup fat
2 cups cooked navy beans
⅓ pound diced American cheese
2 teaspoons chili powder, more or less

Combine the beef, onions, parsley, chives, salt, garlic, and herbs, and put through a food chopper, using the medium blade. Heat the fat, and brown the mixture, stirring frequently. Then stir in the cooked navy beans alternately with the diced cheese, seasoned with the chili powder. When thoroughly mixed and heated through, turn onto a hot platter. Shape like an omelet. Serve at once, dusted with chopped parsley, and surrounded with your favorite tomato sauce.

(4)

## ARMENIAN BURGER CASSEROLE
*Moussaka—serves 6*

2 pounds lean ground beef
1¼ teaspoons salt
1 generous pinch pepper to taste
1 blade each thyme and coriander, ground

1 large eggplant, peeled, sliced (6 slices)
1 tin tomato paste
½ cup bread crumbs
1 scant cup grated cheese

Mix the seasonings with the ground beef. Press the meat in the bottom of a generously buttered casserole as evenly as possible. Over the meat, lay the eggplant slices, which have been spread with the tomato paste. Top with the bread crumbs, and bake, covered, in a moderate oven (350 degrees F.) for 35 minutes. Remove the cover, and continue baking until the bread crumbs are brown. Serve in the casserole with a side dish of grated cheese.

(5)

## BACON AND BURGER GRILL
*Serves 6*

4 strips bacon, chopped fine
1½ pounds lean ground beef
½ pound lean ground pork
1 generous tablespoon parsley, minced
1 generous tablespoon onion, chopped fine

⅛ teaspoon each thyme, sage, mace, and summer savory
1 generous tablespoon chopped green pepper
1¼ teaspoons salt
½ scant teaspoon pepper
12 broiled bacon slices

Combine all the above ingredients, except the bacon slices. Blend well, and shape into 6 cakes. Broil for 5 minutes on each side, turning only once during the broiling. Turn the burgers onto a hot platter, and arrange 2 broiled bacon strips on each. Serve with French fries.

*If a wayfarer in Sumatra sees a little red flag waving on a hut he knows that the family within is eating and there's enough in the pot for guests.*

BAKED BURGER BALLS VEGETABLE DINNER          (6)
  *Serves 6*

1½ pounds ground beef
½ pound lean ground pork
1 generous cup tomato soup
1 tablespoon flour
1 teaspoon salt, or more
⅓ teaspoon pepper, or more
1 pinch each mace, thyme, and basil

¼ cup fat, any kind
1 cup canned or fresh mushrooms, sliced
½ cup chopped onions
1 cup diced celery, blanched
1 cup canned peas
2 cups diced small potatoes
1 cup canned string beans, diced

Combine the meats, tomato soup, flour, salt, pepper, and herbs, and blend thoroughly by putting through a food chopper, using the medium blade. Shape into 18 balls, and brown in the fat. Arrange the meat balls in a buttered casserole, and cover with the mixed remaining ingredients, adding more salt and pepper if necessary. Cover, and bake from 50 minutes to 1 hour in a moderate oven (350–375 degrees F.). Serve right from the casserole.

BAKED BURGER CASSEROLE AU GRATIN          (7)
  *Serves 6*

2 tablespoons butter
1 medium-sized onion, chopped
¼ scant cup flour
2 cups scalded milk
2 pounds lean ground beef
1 tablespoon parsley, minced fine

1 generous teaspoon salt
½ teaspoon pepper
1 blade each thyme, mace, and sage
½ generous cup buttered bread crumbs

Heat the butter. Brown the onion slightly, stirring almost constantly. Stir in the flour, and when thoroughly blended, but not browned, gradually stir in the scalded milk. Combine all the remaining ingredients, except the bread crumbs. Stir into the onion-cream sauce. Cook over a low flame, stirring constantly, until the mixture is thickened. Place in a baking dish. Sprinkle with the bread crumbs, and place under the flame of the broiling oven until the top is a delicate brown. Serve from the baking dish.

(8)

## BAKED BURGER-CHEESE BALLS GOURMET
Serves 6

1½ pounds lean ground beef
½ pound ground cooked ham
1 cup grated cheese
1 large green pepper, minced
1 cup bread crumbs
1¾ teaspoons salt
1 blade each thyme, mace, and nutmeg
⅓ teaspoon pepper
1 teaspoon paprika
1 tablespoon chopped chives
1 tablespoon grated onion
1½ cups cold milk
1 whole fresh egg and 1 egg yolk, beaten
6 strips raw bacon

Combine the above ingredients thoroughly, except the raw bacon. Form the mixture into 6 balls, flattening each slightly. Wrap each ball in a strip of raw bacon. Prepare 1 generous cup of your favorite tomato sauce. Pour this sauce into a greased baking dish, and arrange the meat balls in the sauce. Cover, and bake for 35 minutes in a moderate oven (350 degrees F.). Remove the cover, and continue baking for 10 minutes longer. Serve as hot as possible.

(9)

## BAKED BURGER IN CORN CUSTARD SQUARES
Serves 6

1½ pounds lean ground beef
1¼ teaspoons salt
1 extra large onion, chopped fine
1 clove garlic, chopped fine
¼ teaspoon thyme
2 tablespoons tomato paste
2 teaspoons butter
1½ cups beef bouillon (or water)
6 fresh eggs, beaten lightly
2 cups canned sweet corn
¾ teaspoon salt, more or less
¼ scant teaspoon pepper

Combine the meat, salt, onion, garlic, thyme, tomato paste, and butter in a saucepan. Add the beef bouillon, or water, which has been heated, and allow to simmer for 15 to 20 minutes. Combine the beaten eggs, corn, salt, and pepper. Butter a shallow baking dish. Pour half the corn mixture into the dish. Spread with the meat mixture and gravy. Pour the remaining corn mixture over the top. Bake for 30 minutes in a moderate oven (350 degrees F.). Serve cut into squares.

In 681 A.D., Emperor Kaou Tsung of China built a tremendous grain storehouse, from which any subject was permitted to take grain in time of need.

(10)

BAKED BURGER CUSTARD
  *South African method—serves 6*

### Meat Mixture

2 medium-sized onions, minced fine

2 tablespoons butter

2 tablespoons curry powder

1 scant teaspoon salt

1 generous teaspoon granulated sugar

1 generous tablespoon lemon juice

2 pounds lean ground beef

1 slice bread

1 fresh egg

¼ scant cup milk

Fry the onions in the butter until they begin to color, stirring constantly. Stir in the curry powder, salt, sugar, and lemon juice. Blend well, then stir in the ground beef alternately with the bread slice, soaked in milk, drained, then beaten to a paste with the egg. Turn the mixture into a generously buttered shallow dish or 6 custard cups.

### Custard

2 fresh eggs, well beaten

¾ cup cold milk

¼ teaspoon salt

⅛ teaspoon white pepper

Blanched almond sticks or halves

Make a custard with the eggs, milk, salt, and pepper in the usual way. Pour it over the meat mixture. Place the dish or cups in a pan containing hot water, and bake for 35 to 40 minutes in a slow oven (300 degrees F.), or until the custard is set. Remove from the oven, and put the almond sticks or halves on top. Serve at once.

(11)

BAKED BURGER BALLS
  *Syrian method—serves 6*

1 large eggplant

Cold water

3 tablespoons salad oil

1 tablespoon finely chopped onion

1 small clove garlic

2 cups tomato juice
1 generous pinch thyme leaves
½ teaspoon salt, or more to taste
1 teaspoon lemon or onion juice
1 pound lean ground beef

2 tablespoons salad oil
½ teaspoon salt
⅛ teaspoon pepper
Buttered bread crumbs

Peel the eggplant, and cut into 6 even slices. Soak the slices in cold water for 25 to 30 minutes. Drain thoroughly. Heat the 3 tablespoons of salad oil to the smoking point. Lay in the eggplant slices, onion, and garlic. Brown the eggplant on both sides. Then pour over the tomato juice and thyme, and season with salt to taste. Bring to a boil once. Add the lemon or onion juice to the ground beef and remaining salt and pepper, and form into small balls. Heat the 2 tablespoons of salad oil, and brown the meat balls on all sides. Do not cook them too much; the inside should be rare. Put 3 eggplant slices and sauce in a deep oiled baking dish. Arrange the meat balls on top. Cover them with the remaining 3 eggplant slices and sauce. Then cover with the bread crumbs, and bake until they are a deep brown, in a very hot oven (425 degrees F.). Serve at once with a side dish of plain boiled rice.

**(12)**

BAKED BURGER GEMS WITH TOMATO SAUCE
*Serves 6—individual molds*

Mix the following ingredients: 1½ cups of bread crumbs, 1½ pounds of lean ground beef, 2 medium-sized onions, chopped fine or grated, 2 whole fresh eggs added one at a time, 3 tablespoons of catsup, ¼ teaspoon each of thyme leaves, ⅛ teaspoon each of mace, rosemary, and crushed coriander, 1 scant teaspoon of salt, and ½ generous teaspoon of pepper. Blend well. Divide the mixture into buttered gem pans, and bake about 25 to 30 minutes in a moderate oven (350 degrees F.), or until a delicate brown and the gems leave the sides of the pan. Unmold. Dress on a platter lined with generously buttered spinach. Serve a side dish of your favorite tomato sauce.

*In 1707, a Lord Corwan had built in London a dining table capable of seating fifty guests, with special chairs, each bearing the name and coat of arms of a friend.*

(13)

BAKED BURGER HOME STYLE
*Serves 6*

3 tablespoons of fat, any kind
1 large onion, chopped fine
1 pound lean chopped beef
1 stalk celery, chopped fine
1 No. 2 can tomatoes
1 can mushroom buttons, whole

½ package noodles, cooked
1 generous teaspoon salt
¼ generous teaspoon pepper
¼ generous teaspoon thyme
leaves

Brown the mixed chopped beef and onion in the fat in a hot skillet, breaking it apart with a fork. Add the remaining ingredients, and mix thoroughly. Turn the mixture into a greased casserole, and bake for 35 minutes in a moderate oven (325–350 degrees F.). Serve from the casserole.

(14)

BAKED BURGER AND MUSHROOMS AU GRATIN
*Serves 6*

Let 1 pound of fresh mushrooms soak in 1 quart of water, to which 1 tablespoon of vinegar has been added, for 15 minutes. Meanwhile, heat 3 tablespoons of butter or other shortening, and add to it 1½ pounds of ground beef. Cook until browned through and through, breaking into small pieces with a fork. Then add the drained sliced mushrooms and 2 medium-sized onions, grated. Season to taste with salt and pepper, and continue cooking over a low flame for about 5 minutes. Turn the mixture into a generously buttered or greased baking dish. Cover with, and mix well with, 2 cups of your favorite medium white sauce. Sprinkle with ½ generous cup of grated cheese. Bake for 20 minutes, or until the top is bubbling and brown, in a moderate oven (350 degrees F.). Serve from the baking dish.

(15)

BAKED BURGER AND ONION SHORTCAKE
*Serves 6*

Combine and mix well 1½ pounds of lean ground beef with ⅓ cup of undiluted evaporated milk. Season with salt and pepper to taste, and also ¼ teaspoon each of thyme leaves and mace. Shape into 2 flat round cakes. Spread each with 1 tablespoon of prepared mustard. Then sprinkle with 1 tablespoon of finely minced parsley.

Peel and cut 5 medium-sized onions into thin slices, and separate in rings. Arrange the meat cakes in a greased baking pan or casserole in shortcake fashion, with sliced onions between the layers of meat and on top. Sprinkle with salt and pepper to taste. Dot with 3 tablespoons of ham or bacon fat, or any other fat desired, and bake in a moderate oven (350 degrees F.) for 25 minutes. Then cover, and continue baking for 15 minutes longer, to smother the onion. Serve in the casserole or baking dish, cut in slivers.

(16)

## BAKED BURGER PIE IN PUMPKIN CRUST
*New England method—serves 6 generously*

Select 1 medium-sized pumpkin. Scrub the outside. Cut off about 2 inches from around the top, leaving 2 scant inches of stem, as this cutoff piece is to be used as a cover, the stem being the knob or handle. Remove all the seeds and fibrous matter. Wipe the inside of the pumpkin with a damp cloth. Set aside.

Combine and mix thoroughly 1 pound of lean ground beef; 1 pound of lean ground pork; 2 cups of moistened bread cubes, 3 whole fresh eggs, well beaten; 1 cup of celery, cut very small, using leaves and stalks; 1 large onion, chopped very fine; 1 clove of garlic, minced very fine; 3 tablespoons of butter; salt and pepper to taste; 1 generous teaspoon of poultry seasoning; ¼ teaspoon of thyme leaves; and ½ teaspoon of marjoram. When thoroughly blended, fill the pumpkin with this mixture, and lay across 3 or 4 slices of bacon. Adjust the pumpkin cover. Place the filled pumpkin in a roasting pan. Pour around it 2 cups of canned beef bouillon, or water, and bake in a moderate oven (350 degrees F.) for about 2 hours.

To serve, cut the hot pumpkin pie into wedges or slices. Scoop out the meat mixture, and serve with a side dish of your favorite mushroom or tomato sauce.

(17)

## BAKED BURGER STEAK STUFFED WITH EGGS
*Serves 6*

Combine 1½ pounds of lean ground beef; 2 cups of small bread cubes, soaked in cold milk, then gently squeezed; 1 medium-sized onion, chopped fine; ¾ teaspoon of salt; ¼ teaspoon of pepper; ¼ teaspoon each of thyme leaves, mace, and marjoram; 1 tablespoon of parsley, chopped; 1 blade of garlic, chopped fine; 2 teaspoons of Worcestershire sauce; and 2 whole fresh eggs, beaten. Blend thoroughly. Place the mixture on a sheet of wax paper, spread as for jelly roll. Place in the center 1 cup of chopped hardcooked eggs, mixed with a little white sauce, and roll up. Arrange 4 hard-cooked egg halves, end to end, across the middle of the meat roll. Place the meat roll in a baking dish or casserole. Pour over it 1 cup of mushroom soup, to which has been added ½ cup of onion, minced very fine, 1 generous tablespoon of butter, and salt and pepper to taste. Bake in a moderate oven (350 degrees F.), covered, for about 1½ hours, basting frequently with the mushroom sauce. Serve in slices, cut crosswise.

You may omit the egg filling, rolling up the meat mixture, and placing on top the hard-cooked eggs. Or you may place the hard-cooked eggs inside, instead of the chopped hard-cooked egg mixture.

(18)

BARBECUED INDIVIDUAL BURGER LOAVES
*Serves 6*

Combine and mix well 1 pound of ground lean beef; ½ pound of ground lean pork; 1½ tablespoons of chopped parsley; 1½ tablespoons of chopped onion; 1½ tablespoons of chopped green pepper; 1 generous teaspoon of salt; ½ teaspoon of paprika; ¼ teaspoon of pepper; 1 generous pinch each of thyme leaves, sage, marjoram, and nutmeg; ⅓ cup of bread crumbs; 1 blade of garlic, chopped fine; and ½ cup of cold sweet milk. Shape into 6 individual loaves, and place in a shallow buttered baking dish.

*Sauce.* Combine and mix ½ cup of tomato catsup, ¼ cup of cider vinegar, 2 teaspoons of Worcestershire sauce, ½ small clove of garlic, crushed, 1 tablespoon of grated onion, ½ teaspoon of chili powder, and ½ generous teaspoon of salt. Pour this barbecued sauce over the burger loaves, and bake in a moderate oven (375 degrees F.) for 30 to 35 minutes, basting frequently. Serve hot, each loaf crossed with a broiled strip of bacon.

*Note.* Burger patties may be prepared in this manner.

*Before bringing food to the table, eleventh-century Norwegian homemakers placed it on highly polished shields, so that any devils lurking about would enter the reflection and not the food itself.*

BARBECUED BURGER PATTIES I
*Simmered method—serves 6*

Soak ½ cup of soft bread crumbs in ¼ cup of sweet milk. Combine and mix well with 1 pound of lean ground beef. Season with ¾ teaspoon of salt, ⅓ teaspoon of pepper, and 1 generous blade each of thyme and mace. Blend thoroughly, and form in 6 patties. Brown on both sides in 3 tablespoons of fat.

*Sauce.* Mix together 2 tablespoons of Worcestershire sauce, a few drops of Tabasco sauce, 1 tablespoon of brown sugar, 1½ tablespoons of wine vinegar, ½ cup of tomato catsup, 1 blade of garlic, 1 tablespoon of grated onion, and 1 tablespoon of tomato paste. Pour over the patties. Cover, and simmer very slowly about 10 to 15 minutes, or until the barbecue sauce is thick. Serve as hot as possible, on toast or toasted buns, or on a bed of creamed spinach or mashed potatoes.

BARBECUED BURGER PATTIES II
*Broiled method—serves 6*

Combine 1½ pounds of lean ground beef; ⅓ cup of soft bread crumbs; 1 whole egg, well beaten with 1 extra egg yolk; 1¼ teaspoons of salt; ⅓ teaspoon of pepper; ¼ cup of hot sweet milk; 1 tablespoon of parsley, chopped; 1 tablespoon of grated onion; 1 sliver of garlic, minced very fine; 1 pinch each of thyme leaves, sage, and nutmeg; and ½ teaspoon each of chopped borage leaves and chopped basil. Blend thoroughly. Form into 6 patties. Broil under the flame of the broiling oven, allowing 4 minutes on each side, if desired rare, and 6 minutes, if desired well done. Dress on a sizzling hot platter. Place a pat of butter on each patty.

*Sauce.* Mix together ½ cup of melted butter, ½ cup of tomato catsup, ½ cup of beef bouillon, a little salt to taste, a few dashes of Tabasco sauce, 1 tablespoon of Worcestershire sauce, ¼ cup of unstrained lemon juice, 1 tablespoon of onion juice, and 1 tablespoon of chopped dill. Bring to the boiling point, and pour over the broiled burger patties. Serve at once.

BURGER ESSENCE I
*Beef essence—formula of Professor W. Yeo*

Grind 1 pound of lean round beefsteak, using the course blade.

Place the meat in a wide-mouthed bottle, securely corked, and let it stand for several hours in a saucepan containing boiling water.

(22)

### BURGER ESSENCE II
*Beef essence—formula of Professor M. Hindhede, of Copenhagen*

Grind 1 pound of round beefsteak, using the coarse blade. Put in a heatproof jar or bottle, securely corked, and cook slowly, simmering gently, over a low flame for 3½ to 4 hours.

(23)

### BURGER EXTRACT
*Beef extract, also called beef tea—U.S. Army Hospital formula*

For 12 persons; for less, reduce the amount of ingredients accordingly.

Infuse ⅓ pound of fresh round of beef, finely ground, in 13 ounces of cold soft water, to which ⅛ teaspoon of salt has been added, as well as 4 drops of muriatic acid (drugstore). Let stand for 1 to 1¼ hours. Strain through a very fine sieve or cloth, and wash the residue with 4 ounces of cold water, pressing the cloth to remove all soluble matter. The mixed liquid will contain all the soluble constituents of the meat. It may be drunk cold or slightly warmed. The temperature should not be raised above 100 degrees F., as at 113 degrees F., a considerable portion of the albumin, a very important constituent, will be coagulated. The liquid thus obtained is of a reddish color, possessing the delicious taste of freshly made beef bouillon.

*The bone box was a sixteenth-century English institution. It was kept beneath the table, and well-mannered diners tossed the bones into it when meat was served.*

(24)

### BRAISED BURGERS IN TOMATO SAUCE
*Serves 6*

| | |
|---|---|
| 1½ pounds ground beef with some fat | 3 tablespoons grated onion |
| 1 generous cup chopped raw potatoes | 2 tablespoons finely chopped green pepper |
| 1½ tablespoons parsley, chopped | ½ small clove garlic, chopped |
| | ¼ teaspoon thyme leaves |
| | ½ teaspoon chopped marjoram |

¾ teaspoon salt, or more
¼ scant teaspoon pepper
⅓ scant cup cold milk

1 whole egg and 1 egg yolk, beaten together
2 tablespoons fat, any kind
1½ cans tomato soup or sauce

Combine all the above ingredients, except the tomato soup or sauce, using enough of the cold milk to make a mixture that can be shaped into balls the size of a large egg. Heat the fat, and brown the burger balls on all sides. Transfer the burger balls to a casserole with a tight-fitting lid. Pour over them the tomato soup or sauce. (If using tomato sauce, add a few dill leaflets to enhance its flavor.) Braise in a moderate oven (375 degrees F.) for 30 minutes. Serve from the casserole.

(25)

## BRAISED BURGERS IN CABBAGE LEAVES
*Parisian method—serves 6*

Mix 2 pounds of lean ground beef; 2 fresh eggs, well beaten; 1 medium-sized onion, grated; 1 tablespoon of chopped parsley; 1 tablespoon of chopped green pepper, 1 small clove of garlic, chopped (may be omitted); 2 tablespoons of celery leaves (tops), chopped; 1 generous teaspoon of salt; ¼ teaspoon of freshly ground black pepper; and 1 scant teaspoon of Worcestershire sauce. Blend thoroughly. Shape into 6 sausage forms. Set aside.

Cut off 6 large leaves from a cabbage. Wash well. Put in a large pan. Cover with boiling water, slightly salted, and allow to stand for 5 minutes, or until the leaves are tender and may be rolled. Place a burger sausagelike in the center of each leaf, and fasten with a toothpick or thread at both ends and in the center. Heat ¼ cup of butter in a skillet, and brown the cabbage burgers on all sides. Place the browned burgers in a casserole with a close-fitting lid.

Sauce. Melt 2 tablespoons of butter in a saucepan. Add ¼ cup of chopped onion. Cook and stir until the onion is brown. Sprinkle with 2 tablespoons of flour, ½ teaspoon of salt, ¼ scant teaspoon of pepper, and ¼ teaspoon of allspice. Blend well, stirring constantly. Add gradually 1 cup of scalded sour cream, and ¼ cup of tomato catsup, stirring as it cooks over low heat, to prevent lumping. Boil for 2 or 3 minutes until the flour is cooked. Add ¼ cup of sliced ripe olives and ½ cup of canned mushroom buttons. Pour over the burgers.

Cover tightly, and set the casserole in a medium oven (350 degrees F.) for 30 to 35 minutes. Serve dressed on a hot platter, simply garnished with curled parsley.

(26)

### BRAZILIAN BURGER CASSEROLE
*Serves 6*

Combine 1 pound of lean ground beef; 1 whole egg and 1 egg yolk, beaten together; and 5 small sweet-sour pickles, sliced. Blend thoroughly. Set aside while preparing the following. Bring to a rapid boil 1 cup of beef bouillon, or water, and drop rainlike ½ cup of corn meal into it, stirring constantly to prevent lumping. When smooth, add 1 medium-sized onion, chopped very fine or grated; 2 extra large or 4 medium-sized fresh tomatoes, peeled, seeded, then chopped; 1 extra large or 2 medium-sized green peppers, finely chopped; 1 cup of small raw lima beans; 1 generous teaspoon of salt; ¼ teaspoon of pepper; and a bouquet garni, composed of 1 bay leaf, 5 or 6 sprigs of fresh parsley, 1 sprig of thyme, or equivalent of thyme leaves, tied together. Allow this to boil for 15 minutes, stirring frequently to prevent scorching. Combine the meat mixture with this, and turn it into a generously buttered casserole. Place the casserole in a moderate oven (350 degrees F.), covered, and bake without disturbing for 1 long hour. Serve from the casserole.

*In the sixteenth century, traveling Cossacks carried great iron stoves with them, each slung on poles between two horses. Sometimes meals were cooked on these stoves while on the march.*

(27)

### BROILED BURGERS ENGLISH STYLE
*Serves 6*

Combine and mix thoroughly 1¾ pounds of lean ground beef; 1¼ teaspoons of salt, or more to taste; ¼ teaspoon of pepper; ½ cup of celery, finely ground; 1 medium-sized green pepper, finely ground; and 1 whole fresh egg. Divide the mixture into 6 equal parts, and shape in patties, flattening slightly. Make an indentation

in the center of each burger, and place in it a pat of butter. Broil
for 4 minutes on each side. Have ready 3 English muffins, split
open with the fingers (never use a knife), and toasted. Place a
burger on 6 halves of the muffins, which have been generously
buttered. Pour over the burgers the collected meat sauce and
butter from the broiler pan. Serve as hot as possible, garnished with
crisp green watercress.

(28)

## BROILED BURGERS WITH MUSHROOM SAUCE
*Tearoom method—serves 6*

Prepare 6 burgers as indicated in the recipe above (No. 27).
Omit the English muffins. While the burgers are broiling, prepare
the following quick mushroom sauce.

Cook ½ large onion, minced, with 3 slices of bacon, diced small,
and 1 tablespoon of butter, until the bacon is brown and the onion
soft and yellow. Add ½ pound of fresh or canned mushrooms,
sliced, and cook slowly until the mushrooms are tender. Add 1
can of thick tomato soup, salt and pepper to taste, a few grains of
thyme leaves, and a grating of nutmeg. Simmer gently while
broiling the burgers. When ready, pour the sauce over the burgers,
garnish with crisp watercress, and serve at once.

*Note.* For a complete luncheon, you may top each burger with a
freshly poached egg.

(29)

## BROILED BURGERS WITH ONIONS
*Serves 6*

Mix 2 pounds of lean ground beef; 2 tablespoons of parsley,
finely minced; 1 tablespoon of grated onion; a generous grating of
nutmeg; 1¼ teaspoons of salt, or more; and ½ scant teaspoon of
pepper. Blend well. Place on a well-greased broiler rack or oven-
proof platter. Score the top surface of the meat with a knife, and
spread with butter. Broil under high heat for 5 minutes on each
side, less if wanted really rare. After turning, score, and continue
broiling on the other side. For rare burger, broil 5 minutes on each
side; for medium, 6 to 7 minutes; for well done, 8 minutes. Serve
the burgers on smothered onions.

*Smothered Onions.* Peel 2½ to 3 pounds of onions. Slice thin.

Cook in ¼ cup of butter in a large deep skillet for 5 short minutes. Do not brown; turn frequently, almost constantly. Then pour over ½ cup of meat stock, bouillon, or water. Cover, and let simmer slowly for 15 to 20 minutes. Uncover. Increase the heat a little, and allow the liquid to evaporate, turning the onions frequently.

(30)

### BROILED BURGERS SOUTHERN METHOD
*Serves 6*

Mix 2 pounds of lean ground beef, ¼ cup of cream or evaporated milk, ¼ teaspoon of mace, ¼ teaspoon of thyme leaves, 1 tablespoon each of finely chopped parsley, green pepper, and ground raw bacon, 1 teaspoon of salt, or more, ¼ teaspoon of black pepper, and 1 blade of garlic, finely chopped. Blend well. Form into 6 round cakes. Make an indentation in the center of each cake. Broil in the usual way, that is, 5 minutes for rare on each side, 7 minutes for medium, and 8 minutes for well done. Dress the burgers on a hot platter, and fill each indentation with 1 tablespoon of catsup. Garnish the platter with French fried onions.

*French Fried Onions.* The large yellow or Bermuda onion is what you need. Peel 1 pound of Bermuda onions. Cut them crosswise in thin slices. Separate the rings. Cover with cold milk, and let stand about 20 to 25 minutes. Meanwhile, heat deep fat (hot enough to brown a scant one-inch cube of bread in 1 minute). Drain the onions, and dust lightly with flour. Cook in the deep hot fat until golden brown, stirring occasionally with a long fork to separate the rings, which may stick together. Drain on unglazed paper, and sprinkle with salt. Do not cook too many onions at one time, but rather a small batch at a time. Test the fat for proper temperature (360 degrees F.) after each batch is cooked.

(31)

### BROILED BURGER ON TOAST
*Serves 6*

Mix thoroughly 2 pounds of lean ground beef; 1 teaspoon of salt; ¼ teaspoon of black pepper; ½ teaspoon of sage; ¼ teaspoon of thyme leaves; 2 leaflets of tarragon herb, finely chopped; 1 whole fresh egg, well beaten; and 1 scant teaspoon of Worcestershire sauce. Spread on 6 slices of your favorite bread. Dot with butter, and place under a low broiler flame about 8 minutes without turning. Press the center of each toast with a knife handle, and fill the cavity with chili sauce. Serve immediately with French fried potatoes.

(32)
## BROILED CHEESE-BURGER
*Serves 6*

Split long rolls in half, and generously spread each half with equal parts of butter kneaded with prepared mustard. Or spread the lower half lightly, first with butter, then with prepared mustard. Cover the lower half with a well-seasoned burger, made by your favorite method. Top the matching half with a thin slice of cheese. Broil both sides until well browned, then arrange sandwich fashion, and serve dressed on a hot platter, covered with onion purée.

*Onion Purée.* Cook 1½ pounds of onions in water until very tender. Drain and press through a sieve or potato ricer. Melt ¼ cup of butter, add 3 tablespoons of flour, and blend well. Stir into this gradually 2 cups of scalded milk, stirring constantly until creamy and smooth. Stir in the onion pulp. Season to taste with salt and pepper, and spread on a hot platter before placing in the center the broiled cheese-burgers.

(33)
## BROILED SALISBURY BURGER STEAKS
*Individual—serves 6*

Mix 2 pounds of lean ground beef; 1 tablespoon of grated onion; 1 tablespoon of parsley, minced fine; 1 tablespoon of chives, chopped fine; 1 teaspoon of salt; and ¼ teaspoon of pepper. Blend well. Divide the mixture into 6 equal parts, and shape each part into small individual steaks about ½ inch thick. Sprinkle lightly with flour, and then brush each steak with melted butter. Broil about 2 inches below the flame, allowing 5 or 6 minutes cooking on each side, or more, if desired medium or well done. Have ready the following sauce.

*Brown Snappy Sauce.* Barely cover 1 tablespoon of dried mushrooms with boiling water, and let stand for 4 or 5 minutes. Fry 2 tablespoons of diced raw bacon, and when crisp, skim off the bacon dices, and set aside. In the fat remaining in the pan, fry 2 generous tablespoons of finely minced onion, mixed with 2 tablespoons of finely chopped raw carrots. Then skim off the onion and carrot, and add to the bacon dices. To the same fat, adding a little if needed, add 2 tablespoons of flour, and blend thoroughly until the mixture is a delicate brown. Then stir in 1½ cups of meat stock or canned bouillon. Bring to a boil, and let boil for 2 or 3 minutes to remove the rawness of the flour, stirring almost constantly, until the mixture is smooth and thick. Return the bacon-onion-carrot mixture to the sauce, and add the drained mushrooms, cut into small pieces, salt and pepper to taste, and 1 tablespoon of Worcestershire sauce. Pour over the burgers, and serve at once.

(34)

### BROILED SPICY BURGERS
*Serves 6*

Mix 2 pounds of lean ground beef, 2 tablespoons of prepared mustard, 1 tablespoon of Worcestershire sauce, 1 tablespoon of grated onion, a few drops of Tabasco sauce, 1 tablespoon of parsley, minced very fine, and salt and pepper to taste. Divide the mixture into 6 equal parts, and shape into cakes. Make an indentation on each cake, and broil in the usual way to the degree of doneness desired. Dress on a hot platter. Fill the indentation with a mixture of equal parts of prepared horseradish and catsup. Surround each cake with hot tomato sauce. Serve at once.

*In 380 B.C., the city of Athens commissioned the poet Eriknonus to write an ode in praise of Athenian cooking, inns, and home cooking.*

(35)

### BUDGET BURGER STEW DINNER
*Serves 6*

Brown 3 medium-sized onions, finely chopped, in ¼ cup of fat. When delicately browned, stir in 1½ pounds of lean ground beef, and toss with a fork until brown. Pour over 4 cups of boiling water. Blend well, and let simmer for 10 minutes or so. In a stew kettle, put a No. 2 can of tomatoes, 4 grated and diced small carrots, 4 stalks of celery, diced small, 2 generous teaspoons of salt, ½ teaspoon of pepper, and 3½ cups of cold water. Bring to a boil, then add the burger mixture, and let simmer gently over low heat until the vegetables are tender, or about 1 hour. Then bring the stew to the boiling point. Place a colander on top, and rub the following noodle paste quickly through the colander. Boil for 5 minutes, and serve immediately. The noodle paste will curl in the stew. It is delicious and nutritious.

*Noodle Paste.* Combine 2 whole fresh eggs, which have been well beaten, 5 tablespoons of cold milk, ¾ cup of bread flour, ½ teaspoon of salt, and a pinch of white pepper to make a thin paste or batter.

(36)

BUNGALOW BURGER DINNER
*Serves 6*

Melt 3 generous tablespoons of shortening. When smoking hot, stir in 2 large onions, chopped fine. When the onions begin to color, stir in 1¾ pounds of lean ground beef, and cook until the meat begins to brown. Then stir in a No. 2 can or 2 eight-ounce cans of tomato sauce; 1 six-ounce can of mushrooms, cut fine; and 2 dozen ripe olives, sliced fine. Season with salt and pepper to taste and 1 blade each of sage, thyme, and mace. Add a bouquet garni composed of 1 bay leaf, 4 or 5 sprigs of parsley, and 3 or 4 sprigs of green celery tops, tied together with thread. Bring to the boiling point, reduce the heat, and let simmer very gently for 35 minutes.

Meantime, cook 2 packages of noodles as directed on the package, and drain well. Pour the cooked noodles on a hot platter. Pour the meat mixture over the noodles, and sprinkle with ½ generous cup or more of grated American cheese. Serve at once.

(37)

BURGER APPLESAUCE CASSEROLE DINNER
*Serves 6*

Mix thoroughly ½ pound of lean ground beef; ½ pound of lean ground pork; ½ pound of lean ground veal; ¾ cup of bread crumbs, moistened in milk, then gently squeezed; ¾ cup of canned apple-sauce; 2 whole eggs, slightly beaten; 1 tablespoon each of parsley and green pepper, chopped fine, and of grated onion; 1 small clove of garlic, finely minced; ¼ teaspoon of pepper, and 1¼ teaspoons or more of salt. Form into 6 cakes. Roll in flour, and brown in ½ cup of bacon or ham drippings in a heavy skillet. When brown on all sides, turn the burgers into a casserole. Add 1 stalk of celery, chopped; 1 green pepper, chopped; 1 large carrot, chopped; 2 cups of tomato pulp; 3 medium-sized potatoes, peeled and diced small; and 1 cup of beef bouillon or meat stock. Cover, and set the casserole in a moderate oven (350 degrees F.), and bake for 40 to 45 minutes, or until tender. Serve from the casserole with a green salad, or green salad and fruit mixed.

(38)

BURGER BALLS WITH CREOLE SAUCE
*Serves 6*

Mix thoroughly 1¾ pounds of lean ground beef; ¾ cup of soft bread crumbs; 2 tablespoons of grated onion; 1 sliver of garlic, mashed; 2 tablespoons of parsley, finely minced; 1½ teaspoons of salt; 1 pinch each of cayenne pepper, thyme leaves, and mace; and 2 whole fresh eggs, slightly beaten. Form into 6 balls. Dust lightly with flour, and cook in 3 tablespoons of butter or other fat until evenly browned. You may use rendered beef suet, if desired, using enough to grease the pan while the burgers are browning. Then remove the frying pan to a moderate oven (350 degrees F.), after dotting each burger with a little butter. Pour over hot Creole sauce, made as indicated below, and let stand in a moderate oven (350 degrees F.) for 10 to 15 minutes, to mellow and simmer gently. Serve at once.

*Creole Sauce—Quick Method.* Cover 1 medium-sized onion, thinly sliced, and 1 large green pepper, thinly sliced, with water, and cook until tender, or about 10 minutes. Meanwhile, fry ½ cup of fresh or canned mushrooms, sliced, in 1 generous tablespoon of butter or other shortening until soft. Then add the onion and green pepper mixture, drained, and 2 cups of canned tomatoes, juice and pulp. Cook together for 10 minutes over a gentle flame. Stir in 1 cup of condensed tomato soup, 2 tablespoons of minced cooked ham, and 1 teaspoon of Worcestershire sauce. Season with salt and pepper to taste. Remove from the fire, and stir in 1 tablespoon of butter. Pour over the burgers.

*In the 1850's, contending baseball teams dined together before the game, each player putting away a seven-course dinner and a bottle of wine.*

(39)

BURGER BALLS FRICASSEE
*Serves 6*

Mix thoroughly 1¾ pounds of lean ground beef; ½ cup of fine bread crumbs; 1 tablespoon of parsley, finely chopped; 1 table-spoon of grated onion; 1 whole fresh egg, slightly beaten; 1¼ teaspoons of salt; ¼ teaspoon of pepper; 1 tablespoon of Worcester-shire sauce; and ¼ teaspoon each of poultry seasoning and thyme leaves. Shape into 12 balls of equal size. Heat ¼ cup of butter or other fat, and stir in 6 tablespoons of bread flour, stirring con-stantly until the mixture begins to brown. Then stir briskly until it is well browned. Remove from the fire, and stir in a No. 2 can of tomatoes, using juice and pulp, mixed with 3 cups of boiling meat stock, bouillon, or water. Stir until thoroughly blended. Transfer the mixture to a large saucepan or kettle. Bring to a boil. Add the burgers; 3 large potatoes, quartered; 2 carrots, diced; 1 large onion, quartered; 1 cup of canned string beans; a bouquet garni composed of 1 large bay leaf, 6 sprigs of fresh parsley, 1 large sprig of thyme, and 4 green celery tops, tied together; and 2 whole cloves. Cover, and set over a gentle flame to simmer gently for 1½ hours. Serve very hot, after discarding the bouquet garni.

(40)

BURGER BALL AND KIDNEY PIE
*Serves 6*

Lightly brown 1 medium-sized onion, sliced thin, in 2 tablespoons of butter or bacon drippings, and set aside. Combine and mix thoroughly 1½ pounds of lean ground beef; 1 tablespoon of grated onion; 1 tablespoon of parsley, finely minced; 1 small piece of garlic, crushed; ¼ teaspoon each of thyme, mace, and poultry seasoning; 1 teaspoon or more of salt; and ¼ teaspoon of black pepper. Form into 18 small balls, pressing them lightly. Heat 2 tablespoons of fat, and brown the meat balls on all sides. Transfer then to a deep pie dish, in which a cup has been inverted. Clean, wash, and split 8 lamb kidneys, and sear them in a little butter. Add them to the burger balls in the pie dish, with any juice or butter from the pan in which they have been seared. Add the browned onion; 6 hard-cooked eggs, halved after being shelled; salt, pepper, and a dash of cayenne to taste; 1 tablespoon of Worcester-shire sauce; and enough bouillon, meat stock, or water to fill the dish. Tilt the cup a little to let out the air, so the extra gravy can accumulate under the cup. Cover with a rich pie crust, rolled rather thick. Slash 2 or 3 holes in the top. Bake about 1¼ hours in a moderate oven (350 degrees F.). Serve hot or cold from the pie dish. There should be plenty of rich gravy.

### BURGER BALLS À LA MARYLAND (41)
*Serves 6*

Prepare 18 small burger balls as indicated for recipe No. 40, above. Let stand for 30 minutes to mellow. Meanwhile, heat in the top of a double boiler 2 tablespoons of butter. Blend in 2 tablespoons of flour. Gradually stir in 1 cup of scalded milk, mixed with 1 cup of scalded heavy cream, and 1 tablespoon of onion juice. Bring to a boil, and allow to boil for 2 or 3 minutes. Remove from the fire. Stir in 2 fresh egg yolks, one at a time, beating well after each addition. Then add 2 hard-cooked egg whites, chopped fine. Lastly, add the burger balls. Let this simmer, not boil, for 15 minutes. Then serve 3 balls to a portion on crisp buttered toast. Dust each toast with finely chopped parsley. Serve very hot.

*The Scots used place cards as early as 1327. If the guest was of noble birth, a square of parchment bearing his crest indicated where he was to sit. If he was a commoner, a small slab of wood pictured some past deed.*

### BURGER BALLS SWEDISH METHOD (42)
*Serves 6*

Combine 1 pound of twice-ground lean raw beef, ½ pound of lean raw veal, and ½ pound of lean raw pork. Put the combination through a food chopper. Then mix thoroughly with ¾ cup of fine zwieback crumbs, soaked in 1 cup of undiluted evaporated milk and 1 cup of cold water. Fry ¼ cup of grated onion in 2 tablespoons of butter. Mix with the meat mixture alternately with 2 egg yolks, well beaten and seasoned with 1 scant tablespoon of salt, ¼ generous teaspoon of black pepper, ¼ teaspoon of powdered nutmeg, and ¼ teaspoon of powdered thyme. Blend well. Form into very small balls. Fry in 4 tablespoons of butter over a low flame, shaking the pan frequently to brown on all sides. Serve in a ring of mashed potatoes, creamed spinach, French fried onions, or mashed turnips.

(43)

## BURGER BALLS POLISH METHOD
*Serves 6*

Mix and blend well 1½ pounds of lean raw beef, ½ pound of lean raw pork, 2 whole fresh eggs, well beaten, ¾ teaspoon of salt, ¼ teaspoon of black pepper, ¼ teaspoon of nutmeg, and ¼ teaspoon of thyme leaves. Shape into 18 small balls, and brown on all sides in ¼ cup of fat. Transfer the balls into a greased baking dish. Spread over the balls 1 large onion, thinly sliced; 1 large stalk of celery, diced very small; 3 tablespoons of chopped green pepper; and ½ cup of sliced tart apples. Then over this 1½ cups of canned tomatoes, using juice and pulp. Add a bouquet garni composed of 1 bay leaf, 5 sprigs of parsley, 1 generous sprig of thyme, and 1 sprig of fennel. Cover tightly, and bake in a moderate oven (350 degrees F.) for 45 minutes. Serve in the casserole.

(44)

## BURGER BALLS AND SPAGHETTI MEAT SAUCE
*Serves 6*

Brown ½ pound of lean raw ground beef mixed with 1 sliced medium-sized onion in 2 tablespoons of fat, stirring almost constantly. When beginning to brown, stir in 1 large green pepper, finely chopped. Season with salt and pepper to taste, and cook for 3 or 4 minutes, stirring constantly over a low flame. Set this meat sauce aside. Now combine 1¾ pounds of lean raw ground beef; ¼ pound of raw ground beef liver; 1 tablespoon each of grated onion, grated green pepper, and finely chopped parsley; 2 teaspoons of salt; ¼ generous teaspoon of pepper; a few grains of cayenne pepper; 2 teaspoons of Worcestershire sauce; 1 small clove of garlic, crushed; ¼ teaspoon of nutmeg; and ¼ teaspoon of mace. Blend well, and form into 12 balls. Brown the burger balls on all sides in ¼ cup of fat, shaking the pan frequently. Transfer the burgers into a greased casserole. Pour over this the meat sauce, then 1 can of tomato sauce. Cover, and set in a moderate oven (350 degrees F.) for 35 minutes.

Meantime, cook 1 package of spaghetti as directed on the package. Drain well, butter generously, and dress on a hot platter. Over the spaghetti, arrange the meat balls, and the sauce over all. Serve in the casserole.

*Egyptian physicians of 700 B.C. were empowered to inspect the stock of any food merchant and put him out of business if the merchandise was found to be of inferior grade.*

## BURGER BALLS IN RICH TOMATO GRAVY WITH RICE BORDER (45)
Serves 6

Mix 1¾ pounds of lean raw ground beef; ½ pound of sausage meat; 2 whole fresh eggs, slightly beaten; ¼ cup of bread crumbs; 1 medium-sized onion, chopped fine; 2 tablespoons of parsley, chopped fine; 1 clove of garlic, chopped fine; 2 generous teaspoons of salt; ⅓ teaspoon of black pepper; and ½ teaspoon of sage. Blend thoroughly. Shape into 6 balls or cakes, and brown on all sides in ¼ cup of butter. Transfer the burgers into a generously buttered casserole, and pour over them the following tomato gravy.

Combine a 24-ounce can of tomato juice, an 8-ounce can of tomato sauce, and 1 small tin of tomato paste. Stir in 1 scant tablespoon of Worcestershire sauce. Add a bouquet garni composed of 1 bay leaf, 6 sprigs of parsley, 3 sprigs of green celery tops, and 1 sprig of thyme, tied together with thread. Bring to a boil, turn the sauce with the bouquet garni over the burgers. Cover tightly, and set in a moderate oven (350 degrees F.) for 30 to 35 minutes, or until the gravy is thickened. Discard the bouquet garni, and serve in a plain boiled rice ring, dusted with paprika.

## BURGER AND BANANA GRILL (46)
Serves 6

Combine 2 pounds of lean raw ground beef; 2 whole fresh eggs, slightly beaten; 1 tablespoon of parsley, chopped fine; 1 tablespoon of chives, chopped fine; 2 tablespoons of grated onion; 1 clove of garlic, chopped fine; 2 teaspoons of salt; ½ teaspoon of pepper; ¼ cup of shredded bran, soaked in milk, then squeezed slightly; and ¼ teaspoon each of mace and thyme. Blend thoroughly, then put through a food chopper to insure mixing and smoothness. Shape into 6 large cakes or 12 small ones, wrapping each in 1 strip of bacon for the large ones, and ½ strip for the smaller ones. Secure with a toothpick. Brush both sides of the cakes with butter or bacon drippings. Arrange the cakes on the broiler rack, about 3 inches below the flame. Broil for 5 minutes on each side, or until brown. Brush 6 small bananas with melted butter, sprinkle with salt and a few grains of white pepper, and place on the rack. Continue broiling for 5 minutes, or until the bananas are golden brown, puffed, and tender. Serve each burger and banana with generously buttered noodles.

(47)

BURGER BEAN CHILI
Serves 6

Heat 6 tablespoons of fat. Bacon drippings give a nice flavor. Stir in 5 tablespoons of flour. When well blended and beginning to brown, stir in gradually 3 cups of meat stock or canned bouillon, mixed with ½ cup of tomato juice, stirring constantly until smooth and thickened. Set aside.

Fry 1 large onion, sliced very thin, in 2 tablespoons of fat. When beginning to brown, stir in 1½ pounds of lean raw ground beef, stirring and cooking until the meat is lightly browned. Pour the sauce over the meat gradually, stirring almost constantly. Add 2 tablespoons of chili powder. When blended, stir in 2 cans of beans. Heat well, and serve at once.

*Many stoppers of fifteenth-century wine jugs were made in the shape of a man's head, and the headgear denoted the quality of the wine. The best had a king's head and crown. The poorest, no hat at all.*

(48)

BURGER BEAN DINNER I
Serves 6

Combine 1¼ pounds of lean raw ground beef; ½ pound of lean raw ground pork; 1 tablespoon of grated onion; ¼ teaspoon of lemon juice; 1 tablespoon of parsley, chopped fine; 1 small clove of garlic, chopped very fine or grated; 2 scant teaspoons of salt; ¼ teaspoon of nutmeg; ¼ generous teaspoon of black pepper; ¼ teaspoon of mace; and 2 whole fresh eggs. Blend thoroughly, and shape into 6 cakes. Melt ¼ cup of fat in a skillet. Add ½ cup of thinly sliced onions and 1 clove of garlic, very finely chopped, and cook to a light brown. Brown the burger cakes on both sides, and remove. Add 2 cups of canned tomatoes, or juice, 1 tall can of red kidney beans, and 1 tablespoon of Worcestershire sauce. Bring to a boil. Add the burger cakes, buried in the bean mixture. Cover tightly, and set in a moderate oven (350 degrees F.) for 25 to 30 minutes. Serve from the casserole.

(49)

### BURGER BEAN DINNER II
*Texas method—serves 6*

Slice thinly 1 large onion, and cook slowly until beginning to brown, turning frequently in 2 tablespoons of lard, butter, or bacon drippings. Then add 1½ cups of canned or frozen corn; 2 cups of canned tomatoes, using liquid and pulp; 1 cup of meat stock, bouillon, or water; 1 large green pepper, seeded and shredded very fine; 1½ teaspoons of salt; and pepper to taste. Bring to the boiling point, then stir in 1 cup of yellow corn meal, a little at a time, stirring constantly while adding, to prevent lumping. Cook slowly for 20 minutes, stirring occasionally.

Meanwhile, cook 1 pound of lean raw ground beef in 3 tablespoons of fat or oil, until beginning to brown. Stir this into the corn meal mixture, and set aside to cool slightly. Then beat in 2 whole fresh eggs, a few grains of cayenne pepper, 1 generous teaspoon of chili powder, and 6 or 8 sliced olives. Pour the mixture into a generously greased shallow casserole, and bake for 25 to 30 minutes in a moderate oven (350 degrees F.), covered. Serve very hot with red kidney beans.

In 1802, Biller's Hotel was opened in New York City with much talk about "bringing the farm to the city." The restaurant was decorated like a farm kitchen and farm-style meals were served.

(50)

### BURGER BALLS WITH CAPER SAUCE
*Swiss method—serves 6*

Fry 2 medium-sized onions, finely chopped, in 3 tablespoons of butter. Mix thoroughly 1 pound of lean raw ground beef; ½ pound each of lean raw ground veal and pork; ½ cup of bread crumbs, soaked in milk, then squeezed; 2 whole fresh eggs, slightly beaten; the juice of 1 small lemon; 3 anchovy fillets, washed and chopped; 1 scant teaspoon of salt; ⅓ teaspoon of pepper; 1 tablespoon of parsley, chopped fine, and the fried onions. Put the mixture through a food chopper to insure mixing and smoothness, and shape into 18 balls. Place the balls in a saucepan, and pour over just enough meat stock, canned bouillon, or water to barely cover the balls. Season the water with salt and pepper to taste. Add a small bouquet garni composed of 1 bay leaf, 4 sprigs of parsley, and 1 sprig of thyme, tied with thread, and 2 branches of tarragon leaves or the equivalent of dried tarragon. Cook for 20 minutes. Strain off the liquid, and thicken with kneaded butter and flour in equal parts, using about 1 tablespoon in all. Lift or skim off the burger balls, place on a hot platter, and keep hot while finishing the sauce. To the sauce, from which the bouquet garni has been removed, add ½ cup of washed capers and 1 tablespoon of lemon juice. Bring to a boil, and allow to simmer gently for 5 long minutes. Pour the hot sauce, after tasting for seasoning, over the burger balls. Serve as hot as possible.

(51)

## BURGER AND CARROT STEW
*Serves 6*

This stew is nourishing, economical, easy to prepare, and decidedly different.

Brown 1¾ pounds of lean raw ground beef and 1 cup of coarsely sliced onions in ¼ cup of fat in a skillet, stirring almost constantly. Turn the mixture into a stew kettle. Add 2 bunches of carrots or 1 quart of canned carrots, sliced coarsely; 2 cups of canned tomatoes; 1 whole small clove of garlic; salt, pepper, and mace to taste; a bouquet garni composed of 1 large bay leaf, 5 sprigs of parsley, 1 sprig of thyme, 4 sprigs of green celery tops (leaves), tied together; 2 whole cloves; and 1 tablespoon of Worcestershire sauce. Cover tightly, and set in a moderate oven (350–375 degrees F.) for 1 whole hour. Discard the bouquet garni, and serve as you would a stew. You may serve a side dish of plain boiled potatoes.

(52)

## BURGER CASSEROLE DINNER I
*Serves 6*

Brown 1¾ pounds of lean raw ground beef in 3 tablespoons of butter or other fat. Place in a greased casserole, and arrange a layer of meat, a layer of potatoes, a layer of thinly sliced onions, finishing with a layer of meat, and seasoning each with salt and pepper as you go along. Place 1 large bay leaf on one side and 2 cloves on the other. Pour over 1 large and 1 small can of mushroom soup, mixed with 1 tablespoon of Worcestershire sauce. Cover, and bake for 1¼ hours, without disturbing, in a moderate oven (350–375 degrees F.). Serve in the casserole.

*An old Swedish custom on Christmas Eve is for housewives to make grot, consisting of rice boiled in milk and sprinkled with cinnamon. In it, an almond is hidden, and if a single guest receives it, the superstition is that he or she will soon be wed.*

### BURGER CASSEROLE DINNER II (53)
*Serves 6*

Sauté 1 medium-sized onion, finely chopped, in 2 tablespoons of bacon drippings until brown. Add 1¾ pounds of lean raw ground beef, and stir with a fork until the meat is brown, but not cooked. Sprinkle over 1 tablespoon of flour, mixed with 1 generous teaspoon of salt and ¼ teaspoon of pepper, and blend thoroughly. Gradually stir in 2 cups of tomato sauce, which has been brought to the boiling point, and cook for 3 or 4 minutes. Place 1½ cups of cooked rice, seasoned with salt and pepper to taste, in the bottom of a generously buttered casserole. Turn over this the meat-sauce mixture, and top with another 1½ cups of cooked rice, also salted and peppered to taste. Dot with butter, using about 3 tablespoons. Bake for 25 minutes in a hot oven (400 degrees F.), covered. Serve in the casserole.

### BURGER AND CELERY-ROOT LUNCHEON (54)
*Serves 6*

With a side dish of coleslaw, you have a delicious nourishing luncheon or supper.

Boil 3 large celery roots in salted water until tender. Remove the celery roots from the water. Keep the stock hot. Peel the roots, and cut into scant inch pieces. Set aside. Mix 1 pound of lean raw ground beef; ½ pound of lean raw ground pork; 2 tablespoons of onion, chopped or grated fine; and 1 whole fresh egg and 1 egg yolk, beaten together. Then mix with 1 generous cup of milk, ½ cup of cracker crumbs, ¼ cup of sifted bread flour, and salt, pepper, and mace to taste. Blend thoroughly to make a dropping batter, and drop from a teaspoon into the boiling celery stock. Cook until the burger balls come to the top, then skim them. In a saucepan brown 1 tablespoon of flour in 1¼ tablespoons of butter. Add the celery stock, just enough to make a thick sauce, and stir until thickened. Gently stir in the cut celery root and the burger balls. Reheat well. Serve with generously buttered boiled rice, boiled potatoes, or noodles.

(55)

## BURGER CHOP SUEY
### Serves 6

The charm of the most popular old-world cookery will always win praise for thrifty homemakers and smart hostesses. Ravenous appetites, or jaded ones, are tempted by the alluring goodness of chop suey. Pork, veal, lamb, mutton, ham, and beef, as well as chicken, turkey, and sea food, may be prepared in chop suey fashion. This recipe is a crude imitation of Chinese chop suey.

Chow mein is prepared in the same way, substituting Chinese noodles for boiled rice.

| | |
|---|---|
| 4 tablespoons fat, any kind | ¼ teaspoon pepper |
| ½ generous cup grated onions | 3 tablespoons cornstarch |
| 1½ pounds coarsely ground raw beef | 1 teaspoon Chinese brown sauce |
| | 1 tablespoon Chinese soy sauce |
| 1½ cups celery stalks, chopped | 2 tablespoons cold water |
| ½ generous cup stock, bouillon, or water | ½ teaspoon brown sugar |
| | 1 can Chinese sprouts |
| ¾ teaspoon salt | |

Heat the fat, add the coarsely chopped raw beef and the onions, and fry over a bright flame, but do not brown, scorch, or burn. Stir constantly to sear the meat thoroughly. Add the celery and the stock, bouillon, or water. Cover, and let boil for 5 minutes.

Meantime, make a paste with the cornstarch, salt, pepper, brown sauce and soy sauce (both from grocer), water, and brown sugar. Blend thoroughly until smooth. Stir this paste into the meat mixture, then add the well-drained Chinese sprouts. Heat thoroughly, stirring constantly to prevent burning. Serve on a sizzling platter, heaped in mounds in the center, and surrounded with plain boiled rice.

### BURGER CLUB PLATE RING        (56)
*Serves 6*

Combine 2 pounds of lean ground raw beef, ¼ cup of butter or margarine, ¼ cup of grated onions, 2 cups of soft bread crumbs, 1 tablespoon of parsley, chopped fine, 1 scant tablespoon of salt, 2 teaspoons of paprika, a few grains of cayenne pepper, and 1 teaspoon of dry mustard. Blend thoroughly. Put through a food chopper to insure smoothness, then moisten with ⅔ cup of tomato juice. Pack in a generously buttered ring mold. Spread ⅓ cup of tomato catsup over the top of the ring. Bake in a hot oven (400 degrees F.) for 1 hour or so. Serve hot slices on club plates, each with a moist baked potato, a half broiled tomato, some buttered string beans, and coleslaw.

### BURGER COLLOPS YANKEE METHOD        (57)
*Serves 6*

Heat 3 tablespoons of butter, margarine, or lard. Add 1¾ pounds of lean raw ground beef, mixed with 2 tablespoons of grated onion and 2 tablespoons of minced parsley. Brown slowly for about 4 or 5 minutes, stirring constantly. Then add the juice of 1 small lemon, 1 cup of shredded fresh or canned mushrooms, 1¾ teaspoons of salt, ¼ teaspoon of black pepper, ¼ teaspoon of mace, ¼ teaspoon of thyme leaves, and a grating of nutmeg. Blend well. Moisten gradually with 1 cup of meat stock or canned bouillon, or 1 bouillon cube dissolved in 1 cup of boiling water, stirring constantly while pouring. Simmer for about 10 minutes, stirring occasionally. Arrange a ring of fluffy mashed potatoes and mashed turnips, half and half, well buttered and seasoned, around a hot round platter. Fill the center with the burger mixture. Dust with minced parsley, then with paprika, and serve at once.

### BURGER CORN PATTIES        (58)
*Serves 6*

Mix 1½ pounds of lean raw ground beef; 1 cup of drained canned or cooked corn; 2 tablespoons of parsley, minced fine; 2 tablespoons of celery, minced fine; 2 tablespoons of onions, grated; and 2 tablespoons of green pepper, minced fine. Season with 1 scant teaspoon of salt, ¼ teaspoon of black pepper, and ¼ teaspoon each of mace and poultry seasoning. Shape into 6 cakes according to fancy. Roll in flour, then fry in ¼ cup of bacon drippings for 5 or 6 minutes on each side. When done, dress on a hot platter, and pour over Madeira sauce.

*Madeira Sauce—Quick Method.* Peel ¼ pound of fresh mushrooms. Chop the stems, and leave the caps whole. In a covered saucepan, let them simmer gently in 2 cups of rich meat stock or bouillon, or in 2 cups of water, to which has been added 3 bouillon cubes. Allow to cook until the broth has reduced to half the quantity. Heat 2 tablespoons of butter in another saucepan. Add 3 shallots, chopped fine, and ½ small carrot, thinly sliced, and cook over a low flame for 5 minutes. Then stir in 1½ tablespoons of flour, and continue cooking slowly until the shallots are well browned. Strain this into the reduced broth, keeping the mushrooms for later use. Add ½ cup of good Madeira wine, 1 generous teaspoon of finely minced parsley, 1 teaspoon of tomato paste, 1 teaspoon of soy sauce (optional), and salt and pepper to taste. Allow this to simmer for 10 long minutes. Strain through a fine sieve, add the mushroom caps, simmer for 2 more minutes, and pour over the burger. Delicious!

*New York City's famous Liberty Hotel, erected in 1823, is believed to be the first to have employed waitresses to serve luncheon. All waitresses were Indian maids dressed in tribal costumes.*

(59)

## BURGER CROQUETTES
*Economical—serves 6*

Mix ¾ pound of lean raw ground beef, 1 cup of grated raw carrots, ¼ cup of grated onion, 1 cup of fine moist bread crumbs, 1 whole fresh egg beaten with 1 fresh egg yolk, 1 generous teaspoon of salt, ¼ scant teaspoon of black pepper, and ¼ teaspoon each of thyme and nutmeg. Blend well, then divide the mixture into 6 parts, and shape into croquettes. Roll in fine dry bread crumbs, then in milk, or in beaten egg diluted in milk, and again in fine dry bread crumbs. Set in the refrigerator to chill and mellow. When ready to serve, place in a frying basket, and plunge into hot (365 degrees F.) deep fat. Cook until brown. Drain on absorbent paper. Serve with your favorite tomato or mushroom sauce.

## BURGER CUTLETS

(60)

Serves 6

Here is a luncheon or a dinner fit for a king, if followed with a green salad and a fruit for dessert.

Cook 3 tablespoons of chopped onions in 3 tablespoons of butter, margarine, or lard, until the onion begins to turn yellow. Remove from the fire, and set aside to cool slightly. Mix 2 pounds of lean raw ground beef; 1½ teaspoons of salt; ⅓ teaspoon of black pepper; ¼ teaspoon each of mace and nutmeg; ½ cup of bread crumbs; 1 whole egg, slightly beaten in 1 scant cup of evaporated milk; and 1 tablespoon of finely minced chives (parsley may be used, if chives are not available). Then mix well with the onion, and shape into 6 cutlets, not pressing too hard. Roll in flour, then pan-fry in ¼ generous cup of butter, margarine, or lard for 5 or 6 minutes on each side. Dress the burger cutlets, crown-fashion, in the center of a hot round platter. Surround the cutlets with shoe-string potatoes, and serve a side dish of creamed peas.

## BURGER DELMONICO

(61)

Serves 6

Prick 6 sausages, and pan-broil them until well browned, tender, and shrunk. Keep warm. Mix 1¾ pounds of lean raw ground beef; ½ pound of scalded beef liver, grained with a fork, nerves and tubes removed; 1 tablespoon each of grated onion, minced parsley, minced chives, and chopped shallots; 2 teaspoons of salt; ½ teaspoon of freshly ground black pepper; and 1 tablespoon of Worcestershire sauce beaten with 2 whole fresh eggs. Blend well. Form into 6 boat-shaped burgers. Chill. When ready to serve, push into each burger a cooked sausage. Close the opening. Dip in melted butter mixed with a little lemon juice. Then broil for 6 to 7 minutes on each side under the flame of the broiling oven. Dress crown-fashion on a hot round platter. Fill the center with crisp watercress, and surround the burgers with potato puffs.

Potato Puffs. To 1 quart of hot riced or mashed potatoes, add 3 tablespoons of butter, 1 teaspoon of salt, ¼ generous teaspoon of white pepper, 1 teaspoon of onion juice, ½ scant cup of scalded milk, 3 egg yolks, and 2 canned pimientos, drained and minced very fine. Blend well, then force the mixture from a pastry bag onto a slightly buttered baking sheet, using a large fancy tube. Make each puff the size of a small baking powder biscuit, an inch apart. Carefully brush with melted butter, and place under the flame of the broiling oven until delicately browned.

*In the early sixteenth century, Sicilian families dined in chairs with removable food trays instead of sitting at tables. It saved housework.*

(62)

### BURGER DINNER
*Tennessee method—serves 6*

Brown 1½ pounds of lean raw ground beef in 3 tablespoons of fat, preferably bacon drippings, crumbling constantly with a fork. Add 3 medium-sized onions, thinly sliced, and cook for 4 or 5 minutes, stirring occasionally. Then add ⅓ cup of barley, a No. 2 can of tomatoes, 1½ quarts of hot water, 1 scant tablespoon of salt, and ½ teaspoon of whole peppercorns, gently bruised. Cover, and let simmer gently for 40 minutes. Then add 3 carrots, sliced; 3 large potatoes, diced; 3 stalks of celery, diced; 1 teaspoon of Worcestershire sauce; and 1 teaspoon of A-1 sauce. Cover, and allow to simmer gently for 50 minutes to 1 hour, or until the vegetables are tender. Serve in a hot deep platter.

(63)

### BURGER LUNCHEON
*Puerto Rico method—serves 6*

Mix 1¾ pounds of lean raw ground beef, 1½ tablespoons of grated onion, 1½ tablespoons of minced parsley, 1 teaspoon of salt, ¼ generous teaspoon of black pepper, ¼ teaspoon of mace, 1 teaspoon of Worcestershire sauce, and a few grains of cayenne pepper. Blend well, and shape into 6 round cakes, a little smaller than a slice of canned pineapple. Set aside. Wipe 6 slices of canned pineapple with a clean cloth or paper towel, and sauté in 3 tablespoons of butter or margarine until brown on both sides. Keep warm. Wrap 1 slice of bacon around each burger, secure with a toothpick, and broil for 5 to 6 minutes on each side, or until the bacon is crisp and the burger to the desired point of doneness. Place a burger on each slice of pineapple. Crisscross with half slices of the broiled bacon. Serve on a hot platter, garnished with French fried potatoes.

## BURGER DUMPLINGS (64)
*Bohemian method—serves 6*

A variety of dumplings is always found on every truly Bohemian menu.

Mix thoroughly 1½ pounds of lean raw ground beef; 3 slices of bread, soaked in milk, then squeezed gently; 3 slices of bread, cubed small, then fried in butter until crisp and golden brown; 3 whole fresh eggs, beaten with 3 egg yolks; 2 cups of sweet cold milk; ¾ teaspoon of salt; 1 pinch of pepper to taste; and enough bread flour to make a soft dough. Beat well. Form into dumplings the size of a small apple, and boil in slightly salted water or beef stock for about 25 minutes. Serve with melted butter, or serve with a stew.

## BURGER STEAK FLORIDA (65)
*Serves 6*

Mix 2 pounds of lean raw ground beef, 1½ tablespoons of grated onion, 1½ tablespoons of minced parsley, 1 tablespoon of Worcestershire sauce, 1¾ teaspoons of salt, ½ teaspoon of pepper, ¼ teaspoon each of mace and nutmeg, and ¼ cup of bread flour. Shape in one piece about 1¼ inches thick and the length of your casserole. Place in a greased casserole. Dot with 2 tablespoons of butter, and add a bouquet garni. Pour over enough red wine and meat stock in equal parts to barely cover the burger. Place on each side 1 whole orange, quartered, and free from seeds. Cover tightly, and set the casserole in a moderate oven (375 degrees F.) for 35 to 40 minutes. When done, dress the burger on a long hot platter. Arrange the pan-fried orange sections on top, overlapping each other. Discard the bouquet garni; thicken the gravy, if needed; and pour over the burger. Garnish with alternate bouquets of orange sections and crisp watercress. Serve at once.

*Until the year 1451, the lower classes in England were strictly forbidden to serve food on anything but wooden plates. The no-*

bility dined from silver or gold plates, and on rare occasions glass plates, considered even more precious, were used.

(66)

## BURGER FRICADELLE À LA ROMANE
*Serves 6*

Mix and blend thoroughly 2 pounds of lean raw ground beef; 1 cup of chopped raw spinach; ½ cup of soft bread crumbs, soaked in cold sweet milk, then squeeze very gently; 2 tablespoons of grated onion; 2 whole fresh eggs, slightly beaten; 2 teaspoons of salt; ½ teaspoon of pepper; ½ teaspoon of ground nutmeg; ½ teaspoon of mace; and 1 tablespoon of chopped fennel. Divide the mixture into 6 parts, then form into thick round cakes. Make an indentation in the center with the handle of a knife. Dip in olive oil, and broil for 7 to 8 minutes on each side. Remove from the broiler. Fill indentations with tomato catsup, then cover the top surface and the catsup with a generous sprinkling of grated Parmesan cheese. Return to the flame of the broiler, just long enough to melt the cheese. Serve at once with French fried potatoes.

(67)

## BURGER FRICADELLE À LA RUSSE
*Serves 3—for 6, double the amounts of ingredients*

Season 1½ pounds of lean raw ground beef with salt and pepper to taste. Shape into 6 round cakes, rather flat and of uniform size. Set aside. Beat 2 whole fresh eggs and 2 tablespoons of cold consommé, with a pinch of salt to taste. Turn this into a large frying pan, generously buttered, and fry until the edges are lightly browned. Turn and cook on the other side. Keep hot. Cook ½ cup of onions, finely chopped, in 3 tablespoons of butter until beginning to brown, stirring frequently. Then sprinkle over them 1½ table-spoons of finely minced parsley. Stir once, then remove from the fire. With a pair of scissors, cut the egg pancake into tiny shreds, adding them to the cooked onion and parsley. Then divide the shreds into 6 equal parts. Cover 3 of the burger rounds with shreds. Put the remaining meat rounds on top, pressing the edges firmly together as for a sandwich. Fry the burgers sandwich-fashion in rendered beef suet until nicely browned on both sides. Serve with very hot tomato sauce, mixed with an equal part of warm sour cream. During the chive season, substitute them for onion.

## BURGER AND GRATED SWEET POTATO CASSEROLE (68)
*Serves 6*

Peel 6 large raw sweet potatoes, and grate them on a fine grater. Arrange ⅓ of the grated potatoes in a generously buttered casserole or pudding dish. Sprinkle with salt and pepper to taste. Now put 1¾ pounds of lean raw ground beef in a frying pan containing 3 tablespoons of bacon drippings, heated to the smoking point and slightly brown. Stir with a fork to keep the meat separated. Do not allow to brown. Then stir in 2 tablespoons of grated onion, 2 tablespoons of minced parsley, and 1 tablespoon of Worcestershire sauce. Cover the grated sweet potatoes in the casserole with half of the burger mixture. Repeat with a layer of grated sweet potatoes, then meat, seasoning each time with salt and pepper to taste, and ending with a layer of potatoes. Pour over ¾ cup of hot, not boiling, rich meat stock, bouillon, or consommé. Cover tightly, and bake for 45 minutes in a moderately hot oven (375 degrees F.). Serve from the casserole.

*In 1870, Cornelius B. Paulding, a New Yorker, led a movement to eat without knives, forks, and spoons, claiming that by dining with one's fingers the pioneer spirit could be recaptured. Very few people were interested.*

## BURGER AND GREEN PEAS CASSEROLE (69)
*Serves 6*

Melt 3 tablespoons of butter, and fry in it 3 tablespoons of chopped onions, until golden brown, stirring occasionally over a low flame. Stir in 1¾ pounds of lean raw ground beef. Season with salt and pepper to taste, and let begin to brown, stirring with a fork to separate the lumps. Then pour over 2 cups of canned whole tomatoes, liquid and pulp. Cover, and let simmer for 20 minutes. Now add a No. 2 can of green peas, well drained. Stir gently, and bring to the boiling point. Serve in a casserole with a side dish of plain boiled rice.

## BURGER GRIDDLE CAKES (70)
*Serves 6*

A glass of beer will complete this good snack as a light luncheon or even a supper with a green salad and a light dessert.

Very lightly mix with a fork 1¾ pounds of coarsely ground lean raw beef; 1 medium-sized onion, grated; 1 tablespoon each of parsley and chives, finely chopped; salt and black pepper to taste; ¼ teaspoon each of thyme and nutmeg; and 2 teaspoons of Worcestershire sauce. Heat a griddle very hot, and generously grease it with a piece of fat ham or bacon. Then broil the whole burger, flattened to the thickness of half an inch, as you would a pancake, cooking each side no longer than 3 minutes. Turn onto a hot round platter, and cut into pieces the size of an ordinary piece of pie. French fried potatoes are here indicated, or place on toasted slices of bread, slightly buttered, then rubbed with a little garlic.

(71)

## BURGER GRILL EN BROCHETTE
*Serves 6*

Season 1½ pounds of lean raw ground beef with salt and pepper, 2 teaspoons of grated onion, and a dash of A-1 or Worcestershire sauce. Mix lightly with a fork, and make small round balls. Broil under a hot flame until brown on the outside. Broil 6 strips of bacon, cut into short lengths, and sauté some fresh or canned mushrooms. Dip 6 chicken livers, halved, in butter, and broil until brown on the outside. On 6 metal or wooden skewers impale first a burger, then a mushroom, then a piece of bacon, and lastly half a chicken liver. Repeat once more, having a burger at both ends. Dip in butter, and broil for a few minutes under the flame of the broiling oven. Serve on a long buttered finger toast, simply garnished with a slice of raw tomato and plenty of crisp watercress.

*The Portuguese sovereign, Ferdinand I, in 1381 claimed that his food was tasteless unless musicians played as he ate.*

(72)

## BURGER HODGEPODGE DINNER
*Serves 6*

The Indians ate this first, the pioneers adapted it, and we have been eating it ever since. Of course, the Indians did not have canned vegetables or Worcestershire sauce. These are the white man's additions. This is a fine all-in-one budget dish.

Fry 1 large onion, finely chopped, and 1 clove of garlic, chopped very fine, in 2 tablespoons of olive oil, adding 3 slices of bacon, diced small, until the bacon is crisp and the onion slightly browned. Then add 1¼ pounds of lean raw ground beef, and fry until browned, stirring with a fork to separate the lumps. In a stew kettle, put a No. 2 can of tomatoes, juice and pulp, or the equivalent of fresh tomatoes, cut into pieces; 1 stalk of celery, diced small; and 1 small can of mushrooms, halved or quartered, if large. Pour over this enough cold water to barely cover, and let stand for 1 hour. Then add 1 large bay leaf, tied with 6 sprigs of fresh parsley and 1 sprig of thyme, or the equivalent of thyme leaves. Now add the meat mixture and salt and pepper to taste. Stir well to mix thoroughly, then set over a gentle flame to cook very slowly until the celery is almost done. Then add a No. 2 can of corn, 1 can of tomato sauce, 1 can of minced clams with juice, and lastly 4 medium-sized potatoes, peeled and diced small, and ¼ scant cup of Worcestershire sauce. Cook, still gently, until the potato dices are done. Serve at once.

## BURGER À LA KING (73)
*Serves 6*

Patriotic gourmets take issue with the story that Napoleon's chef was the creator of the almost universal sauce à la King. It is a Yankee concoction originated by the famous chef, George Greenwald, who at one time conducted a restaurant in the Flatiron Building in New York City. Greenwald, when a chef at the old Brighton Beach Hotel, planned to create a new dish which would please the owner, E. Clarke King, 2nd. Chicken à la King was the result, and Mr. King thought so highly of it that he gave it to the world.

Mix 1 pound of lean raw ground beef; ¼ pound of meat sausage; 1 whole fresh egg, slightly beaten; 1 scant teaspoon of salt; ⅓ teaspoon of black pepper; ⅛ teaspoon each of nutmeg, mace, and thyme; and 1 generous teaspoon of onion juice. Handling very lightly, form into small balls the size of a walnut. Melt 3 tablespoons of butter, and brown in it the burger balls on all sides. Drain thoroughly, and keep hot.

*Sauce à la King—Original Method.* Slice ½ pound of mushrooms, fresh or canned; 1 large green pepper, seeded and white ribs removed; and ⅓ cup of drained canned pimientos. Sauté the vegetables in 3 tablespoons of butter until tender, but not brown. Drain the butter thoroughly. Have ready 2 cups of medium white sauce (see No. 90). Stir in 2 or 3 fresh egg yolks, one at a time, stirring well after each addition (2 egg yolks will be enough, but 3 make the sauce richer and smoother). Season to taste with salt and pepper and a grating of nutmeg. (Remember that your white sauce has been already salted and peppered.) Lastly, stir in 2 tablespoons of good sherry. Add the burger balls. Stir very gently, but thoroughly. Place the pan over hot, but not boiling, water, and let the mixture mellow, stirring gently occasionally. Serve on freshly made toast.

*The dinner bell is believed to have originated in Sicily about 50 A.D. when a cook pounded on a piece of metal to summon men who were working in a stone quarry.*

(74)

## BURGER MIGNON À LA STANLEY
*Serves 6*

Mix well 2 pounds of lean raw ground beef; ¼ cup of undiluted evaporated milk; salt and pepper to taste; ¼ teaspoon each of clove, sage, and nutmeg; 2 tablespoons of grated onion; 2 tablespoons of chopped parsley; and 1 teaspoon of Worcestershire sauce. Form into 6 patties of equal size. Wrap each patty in a bacon slice, and skewer with a toothpick. Roll the patties in a hot skillet to cook the bacon. Brown the flat sides of the patties, 5 minutes on each side. Peel and quarter 4 small bananas, and brown in butter on both sides. Place the burgers on freshly made toast rounds, the size of the burgers. Garnish the platter with the bananas and watercress. Pour over each "mignon" 1 generous tablespoon of brown sauce.

(75)

## BURGER OMELET À LA TARTARE
*Serves 1*

Make an omelet in the usual way. When ready to fold, place on it 2 tablespoons of lean raw ground beef, seasoned to taste with salt, pepper, and a pinch of nutmeg, and stirred for 1 minute or so in 1 teaspoon of butter over a gentle flame. The meat should be almost rare, but highly seasoned. Fold the omelet, brush with melted butter, and place for a short minute under the flame of the broiling oven to slightly brown. Serve at once.

## BURGER IN PASTRY JACKET    (76)
*Serves 6*

Mix well 2 pounds of lean raw ground beef; 3 strips of bacon, ground; ¼ cup of tomato catsup; 2 tablespoons of grated onion; 2 tablespoons of minced parsley; ¼ cup of soft bread crumbs; 2 teaspoons of Worcestershire sauce; and salt, pepper, nutmeg, and thyme to taste. Make into 12 small rolls, the shape and size of small sausages. Cut out 4-inch squares of ¼-inch-thick plain pastry. Brush each square with prepared mustard, and roll around the burger sausages. Moisten the edges with a little cold water, and press together. Brush the tops with beaten egg yolk, diluted with a little milk. Bake for 15 to 20 minutes in a hot oven (400 degrees F.). Serve very hot with coleslaw.

*In 1584, the George Inn, on the outskirts of London, featured a sixpence dinner, which offered a choice of "beefe, muttyn, pigge, fich, beer, stranj wynnes."*

## BURGER PASTIES    (77)
*Cornish method—makes 6 pasties*

Mix ¼ cup of flour with 1½ teaspoons of salt, ½ teaspoon of freshly ground black pepper, and ¼ teaspoon each of sage, clove, and nutmeg. Sprinkle this seasoning over 1¾ pounds of coarsely ground lean raw beef, preferably chuck. Then add to this 3 lamb kidneys, free from skins and nerves, and coarsely chopped; 2 tablespoons of grated onion; and 2 tablespoons of minced parsley. Blend thoroughly in a mixing bowl.

Heat ¼ cup of bacon drippings to the smoking point, and stir in the meat mixture. Turn into this hot fat 1¾ cups of meat stock or canned beef bouillon, or hot water, to which has been added 2 bouillon cubes, and let simmer for 10 minutes. Then add 1¾ cups of chopped or cubed cooked potatoes. Heat well, remove from the fire, and keep warm.

Have ready enough pastry dough for 2 ordinary pies. Cut the dough into rounds about 5 inches in diameter. Spread the meat-potato mixture not quite to the edge, moisten the edge with cold water, and fold over to make a half circle. Press the edges together with a fork, or crimp with the fingers. Slit the top of each pasty, there should be 6, to let the steam escape. Brush the tops with fresh egg yolk diluted with a little milk. Place on an ungreased baking sheet, and bake about 20 to 25 minutes in a hot oven (400 degrees F.), or until the top crust is a delicate golden brown. Serve as hot as possible.

(78)

BURGER PATTY DEEP-DISH PIE
*Serves 6 generously*

Season 1¾ pounds of coarsely ground lean raw beef with salt and pepper to taste, ¼ teaspoon each of thyme, mace, clove, and nutmeg to taste, 2 tablespoons of grated onion, and 2 tablespoons of chopped parsley. Shape, patting lightly, into small rounds the size of a large walnut. Brown lightly on all sides in 3 or 4 tablespoons of bacon fat or ham drippings. Remove the burgers from the fat. Into the remaining fat, brown 1 large onion, chopped; 1 green pepper, free from seeds and white ribs, and chopped; and ½ cup of parboiled celery, diced small. When browned, add a No. 2 can of tomatoes, the pulp broken a little in the juice. Now add the burger patties. Let stand for a few minutes to mellow, then turn the whole mixture into a deep pie dish. Roll some pastry ¼ inch thick. Make a few gashes for steam to escape. Fit the pastry over the top of the pie dish, and crimp the edges. Brush the top with a little melted butter, or with egg yolk diluted in a little milk, or with plain water. Bake for 20 to 25 minutes in a very hot oven (425 degrees F.). Serve hot.

*When a sixth-century Hungarian objected to his wife's cooking, it was the latter's legal right to lock him out of the house for the night.*

(79)

BURGER PATTIES SHEPHERD'S METHOD
*Serves 6*

Mix 2 pounds of lean raw ground beef; 2 tablespoons of grated onion; 2 tablespoons of chopped green pepper; 2 tablespoons of minced pimiento; 1 tablespoon of Worcestershire sauce; salt and pepper to taste; ½ teaspoon each of sage, clove, and chopped basil; and 2 tablespoons of ground bacon. Shape into 6 patties, and brown on both sides in 3 tablespoons of fat. Arrange the patties on top of 1 can of condensed vegetable soup. Add 1 large bay leaf tied with 4 or 5 sprigs of celery greens (tops). Spread over all 3 cups of mashed potatoes. Crisscross with the blade of a knife. Bake for 25 to 30 minutes in a moderate oven (350 degrees F.). Serve hot.

(80)

### BURGER PATTIES IN POTATO JACKET
*Serves 6*

Mix lightly but thoroughly 1½ pounds of lean raw ground beef; 3 raw carrots, shredded; 2 tablespoons of grated onion; 2 tablespoons of chopped chives; 1 tablespoon of chopped parsley; 1 whole fresh egg, slightly beaten; 2 teaspoons of Worcestershire sauce; and salt and pepper to taste. Shape into 6 round cakes. Roll in 3 raw potatoes, shredded, and pan-fry for 6 minutes on each side in ¼ cup of bacon drippings. Serve hot with a green vegetable, a salad, and a fruit dessert.

*From 1810 to 1820, economical recipes were very popular in America. Originated by Mrs. Stephen Decatur, they were known as "half-pay recipes."*

(81)

### BURGER CASSEROLE DINNER
*Home method—serves 6*

Cook 1 large onion, chopped fine, in 2 tablespoons of bacon drippings for 2 or 3 minutes, stirring occasionally. Then add 1½ pounds of lean raw ground beef chuck, and cook until lightly browned, stirring constantly with a fork to separate the pieces. Place half of the meat, salted and peppered to taste, in a greased casserole. Cover with ½ can of drained peas. Add the remaining meat mixed with the remaining peas. Top with 1 package of noodles, cooked, well drained, and generously buttered. Pour over the noodles 1 can of condensed tomato soup. Bake for 30 minutes in a moderate oven (350 degrees F.). Serve right from the casserole.

(82)

## BURGER DOUBLE-CRUST PIE
*Serves 6*

In 3 tablespoons of heated bacon drippings, sauté ¼ cup of minced onions until slightly colored. Add 1¼ pounds of lean raw ground beef chuck, and cook for 8 to 10 minutes, stirring until the meat is barely colored. Season with 1¼ teaspoons of salt and ¼ teaspoon of black pepper. Pour over 1 can of condensed tomato soup, mixed with 1 tablespoon of Worcestershire sauce and ¼ teaspoon each of thyme, sage, and clove. Simmer about 10 minutes, or until the mixture is well heated, stirring occasionally. Line a 9-inch pie plate with a rich flaky pastry. Pour in the filling. Cover with a top crust. Prick the top with a fork, and brush with melted butter. Bake in a hot oven (400 degrees F.) for 10 minutes to set the pastry. Reduce the heat to 375 degrees F., and continue baking for 30 minutes longer, or until the crust is delicately browned. Serve hot.

(83)

## BURGER TAMALE PIE
*Serves 8 generously*

Stir 1 cup of yellow corn meal into 2 cups of boiling water. When smooth, pour the mixture over 2 slightly beaten whole eggs alternately with 1 cup of sweet milk, scalded, then cooled. Spread ⅔ of the corn meal mixture in a generously greased baking dish, then pour in the filling.

*Tamale Filling.* Brown 2 large onions, chopped, and 1 clove of garlic, chopped fine, in ½ scant cup of cooking oil, stirring frequently. Stir in 1 generous teaspoon of chili powder, then ¾ pound each of lean raw ground beef and pork, mixed together. Brown well. Then add a No. 2 can of corn, a No. 2 can of hominy, a No. 2 can of tomatoes, and 1 cup of ripe olives, chopped; mix all together and season with 2 generous teaspoons of salt. Blend well, and when hot, turn the mixture into the lined dish. Top with the remaining corn meal mixture, and bake for 40 to 45 minutes in a moderate oven (350 degrees F.). Serve hot in winter, cold in summer.

*In the fifteenth century, Dutch gentlemen removed their own and their wives' shoes before sitting down to table. They believed this aided digestion.*

(84)

## BURGER VEGETABLE PIE
*Serves 6*

Heat 3 tablespoons of bacon drippings, lard, or butter; add 1½ pounds of lean raw ground beef chuck with 3 tablespoons of chopped onion; and brown lightly. Then add 3 large potatoes, peeled and cubed small, and 1 cup of grated raw carrots, cubed small. Season with 1 teaspoon of celery seed; 1½ teaspoons of salt; ½ teaspoon of black pepper; 1 tablespoon of parsley, minced; ¼ teaspoon each of thyme, sage, and clove; and if desired, 1 blade of garlic. Stir 2 tablespoons of flour into 2 cups of meat stock or bouillon, or hot water in which has been diluted 2 bouillon cubes, and pour over the mixture. Bring this to the boiling point, then let simmer for 15 minutes. Pour into a greased deep pie dish. Cover with baking powder biscuit dough, rolled ¼ inch thick. Prick the top of the crust with a fork. Bake about 25 minutes, or until the crust is brown, in a hot oven (400 degrees F.). Serve hot.

(85)

## BURGER PLANKED DINNER
*Serves 6*

Mix 1½ pounds of lean raw ground beef chuck, 1¼ teaspoons of salt, ¼ generous teaspoon of black pepper, 2 tablespoons of grated onion, 2 tablespoons of ground green celery tops, 1 tablespoon of chopped parsley, 1 tablespoon of Worcestershire sauce, and ¼ teaspoon each of clove and thyme. Shape into 6 burger cakes. Brush with melted butter, and broil for 5 minutes on each side. Dress on a buttered oak plank, the border of which is surrounded with a ring of fluffy mashed potatoes, forced through a pastry bag with a large fancy tube, sprinkled with melted butter, and golden-browned under the flame of the broiling oven. Arrange the burgers neatly, and in between each burger, arrange little mounds of cooked vegetables, such as peas, generously buttered and sprinkled with parsley, creamed or buttered carrots, cauliflower, asparagus tips crossed with a ring of pimiento, baked tomatoes stuffed with rice, and glazed onions or French fried onion rings. You may pass a side dish of your favorite brown or tomato sauce.

(86)

## BURGER PORCUPINES
*New England method—serves 6*

Combine and mix lightly but thoroughly 1¾ pounds of lean raw ground beef chuck; 1 generous teaspoon of baking powder; 1 medium-sized onion, grated; 2 tablespoons of chopped parsley; 1 scant cup of sweet cold milk; 2¼ teaspoons of salt; ½ teaspoon of black pepper, ½ cup of washed and drained uncooked rice; ¼ teaspoon each of clove, poultry dressing, and thyme; and 1 teaspoon of Worcestershire sauce. Form into 6 balls, flattening both ends a little. Place in a baking pan. Pour over 2 cans of condensed tomato soup mixed with 2 cups of cold water. Bake uncovered in a moderate oven (350 degrees F.) about 35 minutes. Cover, and continue baking for 30 minutes longer. Serve as hot as possible.

*A Mrs. Shortmeal is credited with having been the author of the first cookbook consisting exclusively of New England recipes. It was published in Boston in 1751.*

(87)

## BURGER POTATO SAUSAGE
*Swedish method—serves approximately 6*

These delicious sausages are fine when cold to serve on a tray of hors d'oeuvres or appetizers.

Combine ⅔ pound of lean raw ground beef chuck; ⅓ pound of lean raw ground pork; ⅓ pound of lean raw ground veal; 3 cups of peeled raw potatoes (about 4 medium-sized potatoes), ground or grated; 1 medium-sized onion, peeled, quartered, then ground; and ½ to ⅔ cup or just enough to moisten of meat stock or canned bouillon, or water in which has been diluted, then cooled, 2 bouillon cubes. Season with 2¼ teaspoons or more of salt, ½ generous teaspoon of freshly ground black pepper, 1 generous teaspoon of allspice, ¼ teaspoon of thyme, and ¼ teaspoon of clove. Blend thoroughly, then put twice through a food chopper to insure smoothness and thorough blending. Stuff this mixture into clean, washed, then sponged dry casings, about twice the size of a frankfurter sausage, but not so long, which may be obtained at some markets or a sausage factory.

To facilitate the filling of the casings, use the center of an angel cake tin. Slip the casing over the tube in the left hand, as you fill in the mixture with the right. Fill each casing only ¾ full. Tie up the ends. Place these sausages in rapidly boiling salted water, and cook steadily uncovered, reducing the heat a little, for about 45 minutes. Prick the casings in a few places when first starting to boil, to allow air to escape, thus preventing bursting. Drain. Serve hot on a hot platter covered with creamed spinach, boiled cabbage, fluffy mashed potatoes, sauerkraut, mashed green peas, or mashed turnips.

(88)

BURGER POT ROAST DINNER
*Serves 6 generously*

Mix lightly but thoroughly 2½ pounds of lean raw ground beef chuck; 2 whole fresh eggs, slightly beaten; 2 teaspoons of salt; ½ teaspoon of black pepper; ½ cup of thin cream or undiluted evaporated milk; and ½ cup of cracker or bread crumbs. Put the whole mixture through a food chopper to insure smoothness and thorough blending. Then shape into a loaf, flattening a little the bottom and top. Sear on both sides in ¼ cup of bacon drippings, using a pancake turner to turn the meat. Transfer the meat to a stew kettle with the drippings from the searing. Add 1 small veal bone (about ½ to ¾ pound); a bouquet garni composed of 1 large bay leaf, 6 sprigs of fresh parsley, 4 sprigs of green celery leaves (tops), and 1 branch of thyme, tied together with thread; 1 large green pepper, cut into eighths; 8 whole peppercorns, bruised; ¼ teaspoon of mace; 2 medium-sized carrots, cut into small pieces; 12 small white onions, peeled and left whole; 12 mushroom caps, whole, the stems sliced; and 2 whole cloves. Pour over enough cold meat stock or water to barely cover. Adjust the lid tightly, and set in a moderate oven (350 degrees F.) for 2¼ hours. Carefully dish up the vegetables first on a hot platter, then the loaf. Discard the veal bone and the bouquet garni. Thicken the gravy with a little flour, and taste for seasoning. Strain part of the gravy over the burger and vegetables placed on a hot deep platter. Serve a side dish of plain boiled potatoes, and with a salad you'll have a dinner fit for a king.

When a Malay dined in the nineteenth century, his wife took her position at the open door, where she called loudly: "My man eats. I have made fried meat! My man eats!"

(89)

## BURGER RAGOUT À LA CREOLE
*Serves 6*

Mix 2 pounds of lean raw ground beef chuck; ½ cup of bread crumbs; 2 tablespoons of grated onions; 1 generous tablespoon of chopped green pepper; 2 whole fresh eggs, slightly beaten; 1 tablespoon of prepared mustard; 1 large clove of garlic, chopped fine; 1 tablespoon of wine vinegar; 1 teaspoon of lemon juice; salt and pepper to taste; ¼ teaspoon of mace; ¼ teaspoon of summer savory; and 1 generous pinch of clove. Shape into 6 patties. Heat 2 tablespoons of lard, and fry 1 medium-sized onion, chopped, until it begins to color. Turn the onion and fat into a stew kettle, and lay the burgers on the onion. Add 2 dozen small raw potato balls; 1 dozen small raw carrot balls; 1 bouquet garni; 2 tablespoons of tomato purée; 1 dozen very small white onions, peeled and left whole; 2 whole cloves; enough meat stock, bouillon, or water to barely cover; and 6 whole peppercorns. Adjust the lid tightly, and place in a moderate oven (325 degrees F.) for 2 hours without disturbing. Remove the burgers very carefully onto a hot platter, then the vegetables. Discard the bouquet garni. Taste for salt, if needed. Thicken the gravy, if necessary. Then strain part of the gravy over the burgers and vegetables. Serve the remaining gravy aside.

(90)

## BURGER RAREBIT
*Serves 6*

Blend ¼ pound of grated American cheese with 1¼ cups of hot medium white sauce, stirring well until the cheese is melted. Add 1¼ teaspoons of dry mustard, or more according to taste, and a few drops of Worcestershire sauce. Pour over broiled burger patties, placed on freshly made rounds of toast. Garnish with parsley or watercress, ripe olives, and sliced tomato.

*White Sauce.* White sauce is made in varying degrees of thickness depending on its use. *Thin white sauce* is used as a base for cream soups. It is made with 1 tablespoon each of butter and flour to 1 cup of milk. *Medium white sauce* is used for eggs, fish, meat, poultry, and vegetables, and as a base for soufflés. It is made with 1½ or 2 tablespoons each of butter and flour to 1 cup of milk.

*Thick white sauce* is used for croquette mixtures, also for some soufflés. It is made with 3 or 4 tablespoons each of butter and flour to 1 cup of milk. Always use equal parts of butter and flour for best results, unless otherwise indicated. Use ¼ teaspoon of salt to the above quantities for thin and medium white sauce, and ½ teaspoon of salt for the thick sauce. A dash of white pepper in all three sauces.

Melt the butter. Add the flour mixed with the salt and pepper. Stir until well blended, but not browned at all. Add the milk gradually, while stirring constantly over moderate heat. Continue to stir until the mixture is thick and smooth.

*An old Irish custom that lasted until about 1860 was for green-grocers to decorate their stores with four-leaf clovers. This was supposed to keep the food from going bad before it was sold.*

(91)

## BURGER À LA RAVENNA
*French method—serves 6*

Mix well but lightly 2 pounds of lean raw ground beef chuck; 2 tablespoons of chopped shallots; 2 tablespoons of chopped chives; 2 tablespoons of chopped parsley; 1 large clove of garlic, grated; 2 whole fresh eggs, slightly beaten; 3 tablespoons of tomato catsup; 2 teaspoons of Kitchen Bouquet; 2 teaspoons of salt; ½ teaspoon of freshly ground black pepper; a dash of Tabasco sauce; and ½ teaspoon of dried tarragon herb leaves. Shape into 6 cakes, flattening lightly, and broil for 5 short minutes on each side. Place the burgers in a generously buttered baking pan, then pour over 2 cups of red wine. Cover the pan, and cook over a medium flame for about 10 minutes. By that time, the red wine has been reduced about half, and the juices of the meat have become well mixed with it. Now remove the burgers to a hot platter. Thicken the gravy with 1 teaspoon of butter and 1 teaspoon of flour, kneaded together. Bring to the boiling point, and let simmer for 1 minute or so. Just before pouring the sauce over the burgers, add to it a dash or two of Kitchen Bouquet. Correct the seasoning. Serve immediately with hashed browned potatoes and broiled thick tomato slices.

BURGER RICE CABBAGE ROLLS
*Turkish method—serves 6*

Combine and mix well but lightly 1½ pounds of lean raw ground beef chuck, 1 cup of cooked and well-drained cold rice, salt and pepper to taste, a few grains of cayenne pepper, 2 tablespoons of grated onion, and 1 teaspoon of Kitchen Bouquet. Set aside. Cover 12 nice cabbage leaves with slightly salted boiling water. Let stand for 4 or 5 minutes. Drain and sponge the cabbage leaves, and dry with a clean dry towel. Spread the leaves on a wet board, and trim them neatly to the same size. Place on each cabbage leaf 1 or 2 tablespoons of the burger mixture. Roll up like a jelly roll, and tie with thread at both ends. Place the cabbage rolls close together in a generously buttered or oiled baking pan. Pour over 1 cup each of canned tomatoes and sour thick cream, seasoned to taste with salt and pepper. Place a buttered paper on top, and bake for 35 minutes in a moderate oven (375 degrees F.). Serve 2 rolls to a portion.

*Variation.* Instead of tomatoes and sour cream, pour over 2 cups of brown gravy or sauce, highly seasoned, and proceed as indicated.

(93)

BURGER AND RICE CASSEROLE DINNER
*Serves 6 generously*

Heat ¼ cup of bacon or ham fat, or olive oil or other cooking oil, to the smoking point. Brown in it ¾ cup of well-washed, well-drained uncooked rice, stirring almost constantly, for about 10 minutes, adding more fat as soon as the rice turns yellow through the absorption of the fat. Then stir in 1½ pounds of lean raw ground beef chuck for about 5 minutes. Transfer the mixture to a greased casserole. Stir in 1 cup of thinly sliced onion; 1 clove of garlic, finely chopped; ½ cup of celery greens (tops), chopped; 1 large bay leaf tied with 6 sprigs of fresh parsley; 2 whole cloves; 2 teaspoons or more of salt; ½ teaspoon of black pepper; and 2 teaspoons of curry powder, all stirred into 2 cups of tomato soup. Place on the top 6 strips of bacon. Adjust the cover tightly, and bake for 1½ hours in a moderate oven (375 degrees F.) without disturbing. Serve right from the casserole.

*In the thirteenth century, Scottish noblemen used napkins made from sheep's hide. By beating the hide for a long period and using a secret process, the napkin was made soft as linen.*

## BURGER RING MOLD DINNER
(94)

*Serves 6*

Mix well but lightly 1½ pounds of lean raw ground beef chuck; ½ pound of lean raw ground pork; ½ pound of lean raw ground veal; 1 scant tablespoon of salt; ½ generous teaspoon of black pepper; ¼ cup of grated onion; 2 tablespoons of minced parsley; 1 tablespoon of Worcestershire sauce; 2 whole fresh eggs, slightly beaten with ¼ cup of tomato catsup; and ¼ teaspoon each of thyme, sage, and mace. Pack the mixture into a generously greased ring mold. Sprinkle over it 4 strips of raw bacon, ground. Cover with a buttered paper, and bake in a moderate oven (375 degrees F.) about 1 hour. Remove the paper, and continue baking for 15 minutes longer, or until the ground bacon is crisp. Remove from the oven. Invert, and let stand for 1 minute or so. Then lift off the mold. Fill the center with canned or freshly made baked beans, heated. Garnish the platter with parsley and ripe olives.

## BURGER ROLLS LUNCHEON
(95)

*Serves 6*

Mix 1½ pounds of lean raw ground beef chuck, 6 tablespoons of thick sour cream, 2 tablespoons of grated onion, 1½ teaspoons of salt, ¼ teaspoon of black pepper, 1 tablespoon of minced parsley, and 1 teaspoon of Worcestershire sauce. Shape into 6 small loaves. Wrap 1 long strip of bacon around each loaf diagonally, so that the bacon reaches from one end to the other. Run a skewer through lengthwise, catching each end of the bacon strip. Place on the broiler rack, and broil for 6 to 7 minutes on each side. Dress the loaves in the center of a hot platter, and surround with 6 stuffed green peppers.

*Stuffed Green Peppers.* Select 3 large green peppers of equal size. Wash carefully; sponge dry; split in half crosswise; and remove the seeds and white ribs thoroughly. Then scald them for 5 short minutes to render them more tender. Mash ½ pound of cottage cheese with a fork to a creamy consistency. Stir in ½ generous teaspoon of salt, 1 tablespoon of grated onion, ¼ teaspoon of paprika, and a dash of Worcestershire sauce. Fill the green pepper halves with this mixture. Top with ½ cup of buttered crumbs, for 6 peppers. Place in a greased baking pan with ½ cup of tomato juice, bouillon, meat stock, or water in the bottom. Bake in a moderate oven (350 degrees F.) for 20 minutes, beginning to baste after 15 minutes of baking. Delicious, and nutritious too.

*In 221 A.D., Lucius of Rome ran a successful chain of sixteen groceries, which sold graded vegetables in various-sized packages.*

(96)

BURGER ROLY-POLY WITH OLIVE SAUCE
*Serves 6*

*Biscuit Dough.* Mix and sift together twice 2 cups of bread flour, 3 teaspoons of baking powder, 1 teaspoon of salt, and a few grains of cayenne pepper to taste. Cut in ¼ cup of shortening. Add ¾ scant cup of cold sweet milk, stirring quickly to make a soft dough. Turn onto a lightly floured board. Knead slightly, and roll into a rectangle a scant half inch thick.

*Burger Filling.* Season 1½ pounds of lean raw ground beef chuck with 1¼ teaspoons of salt, ¼ teaspoon of black pepper, 1½ tablespoons of grated onion, 1 tablespoon of minced parsley, 1 teaspoon of Worcestershire sauce, ¼ teaspoon of dry mustard, and 3 tablespoons of melted bacon drippings. After blending thoroughly but lightly, spread on the biscuit dough, and roll as for jelly roll. Cut in slices 1½ inches thick. Place on a generously greased baking sheet, and bake for 20 to 25 minutes in a hot oven (425–450 degrees F.).

*Olive Sauce.* To 1 cup of Brown Snappy Sauce (see No. 33), add ½ cup of pitted sliced ripe olives. Bring to the boiling point, and serve.

(97)

BURGER ROLY-POLY WITH RAISIN SAUCE
*Without biscuit—serves 6*

The raisin sauce in this recipe is Southern, and is excellent also with ham.

*Burger Wrapper.* Mix thoroughly but lightly 1 pound of lean raw ground beef; ½ pound of lean raw ground veal; ½ pound of lean raw ground pork; 2 whole fresh eggs, slightly beaten; 2 table-spoons of grated onion; 1 tablespoon of chives, finely chopped; 2 teaspoons of salt; ½ teaspoon of black pepper; 3 tablespoons of melted ham fat. Place this mixture on a board, slightly wet, and very lightly roll it out, forming a rectangle half an inch thick.

*Filling.* Mix 1½ cups of fine dry bread crumbs; 2 tablespoons of finely chopped onion; ½ cup of chopped green celery tops; ½ tea-spoon of thyme leaves; ½ generous teaspoon of salt; ¼ teaspoon of black pepper; ½ teaspoon of sage; ½ cup of chopped green pepper; ¼ pound of meat sausage, slightly browned in its own fat, stirring while browning to separate the lumps; and 2 tablespoons of bacon drippings.

Spread the filling on the burger wrapper, and roll as for jelly roll. Place in a greased roasting pan large enough to hold it easily, but not too large. Bake for 1½ hours in a moderate oven (325 degrees F.), basting frequently with hot water mixed with a little butter. Dress on a hot platter. Surround with broiled tomato slices, and serve with a side dish of raisin sauce.

*Raisin Sauce.* Cover ½ cup of seedless raisins with water. Add 3 cloves, and bring to the boiling point. Reduce the flame, and let simmer for 10 minutes, covered. Then add ⅓ cup of brown sugar, ½ scant teaspoon of cornstarch, and salt and pepper to taste. Stir until the sauce is slightly thickened, then add 1 tablespoon of butter, ½ teaspoon of vinegar, and a few drops of Worcestershire sauce. Pour the sauce over the roly-poly.

*Broiled Tomato Slices.* Select 3 firm, not too ripe tomatoes. Wash, remove the stem end, but do not peel. Cut in half, and make crisscross cuts on the top of each half with a knife. Dip the slices in melted butter, seasoned with a little lemon juice and salt and pepper to taste. Place on a greased broiler, and broil under moderate heat about 4 minutes on each side, or until lightly browned and tender. Place around the roly-poly. Between the to-mato slices, place some crisp parsley or watercress.

> Great Grandma when the West was new,
> Wore hoop skirts and a bustle, too;
> But when Injuns came and things looked bad,
> She fit right in alongside Great Granddad.
> She worked hard seven days in the week
> To keep Granddad well fed and sleek;

She biled the beans, and she hung out the wash,
And she never had time to drink tea, by gosh.
Twenty-one necks she had to scrub,
Wash twenty-one shirts in the old washtub,
Cook twenty-one meals three times a day;
No wonder Grandma's hair turned gray.
She worked all day, and she slept all night,
Which, it seems to me, is just about right;
With great granddaughter it's the other way,
She's up all night, and she sleeps all day.
OLD WESTERN SONG

(98)

## BURGER SANDWICH GRILL
Serves 6

For 6 good-sized sandwiches, mix 1½ pounds of lean raw ground beef chuck, ⅓ cup of sweet cold milk, 2 tablespoons of grated onion, 1½ teaspoons of salt, ⅓ teaspoon of black pepper, 1 tablespoon of Worcestershire sauce, and 1 tablespoon of tomato catsup. Divide the mixture into 6 equal parts. Spread generously on 6 slices of buttered bread, which may be spread first with a film of prepared mustard. Spread the burger mixture right to the edges to cover the crusts. Place on the broiler rack, or use a cake cooling rack in a shallow baking pan. Broil for 4 or 5 minutes, or longer, according to the degree of doneness desired. Put a thick onion slice on each sandwich, dot with butter, sprinkle with salt and pepper to taste, and broil until the onion begins to brown. The onion slices should be almost raw to enjoy their full flavor. Serve immediately.

(99)

## BURGER AND SAUERKRAUT BALLS
Serves 6

Sauerkraut is an age-old food, which did not originate in Germany, as is commonly believed. It dates back to the building of the Great Wall of China, when the laborers ate it to combat deficiency diseases resulting from a diet consisting almost altogether of rice. Originally, the Tartars introduced the acid cabbage from the Orient into eastern Europe, and from there it went to Alsace and Lorraine, which is not Germany.

It is recommended that kraut and fatty meats should not be cooked too long together, otherwise the grease will penetrate the kraut and decrease the lactic ferments. So many good things can be done with kraut. Tuck frankfurters into the sauerkraut, and cook until they hiss from the heat. Put sauerkraut in a baking dish with a layer of spareribs on top, and bake in a moderate oven, turning the ribs to get them cooked through and crackling brown on both sides. Serve sauerkraut with loin or shoulder of pork, and scalloped sauerkraut with macaroni and shredded bits of smoked ham.

Salt turns shredded cabbage into kraut. It draws out the cabbage juice, which contains sugar. This ferments and lactic acid forms, giving that faint tangy flavor and distinctive texture that stimulates the appetite and makes kraut kraut the world around. Properly cooked, kraut loses virtually none of its health properties and is considered on a par with the raw product.

Combine ¾ pound of lean raw ground beef; ¾ pound of lean raw ground pork; ½ pound of lean raw ground veal; 3 slices of bread, soaked in 1 scant cup of milk; 2 tablespoons of grated onion; 2 tablespoons of chopped parsley; salt, pepper, and cayenne pepper to taste; and 2 whole fresh eggs, slightly beaten. Mix thoroughly but lightly. Form into 12 flat cakes.

Mix 4 pounds of sauerkraut, 1 teaspoon of caraway seeds, 2 crushed bay leaves, and 8 whole cloves. Divide into 4 parts. In a kettle, place a layer of kraut, then 3 burger cakes. Repeat until all are used, having the top layer kraut. Add 1 pint of hot water, or enough to barely cover. Simmer, covered, for 2 hours, adding more boiling water if necessary. Serve with plain boiled potatoes and rye bread.

*In Italy in the seventh century, a man could sign a contract with an innkeeper to feed him for the entire year for the equivalent of about $32.*

(100)

## BURGER SCRAMBLED EGGS
### Serves 1

Scramble 2 eggs in the usual way. When they are beginning to get firm, stir in 6 ounces of lean raw ground beef, seasoned to taste with salt and pepper. Serve on freshly made buttered toast.

## BURGER SHORTCAKE I
*Serves 6*

When the nation was younger, the mixing bowl was a common kitchen utensil. It was a big yellow bowl. Into it went flour and milk, sugar and yeast, fat and salt—but something more. There was the touch of the artist that produced the bread, biscuits, and pies.

Biscuits need a hot oven (450 degrees F.), and naturally the smaller they are, the quicker they will bake. As soon as they are out of the oven, they should be served, so that the butter will melt when they are split and buttered.

*Baking Powder Biscuits.* Sift 2 cups of bread flour twice. Return to the sifter, add 1 tablespoon of baking powder and ½ generous teaspoon of salt, and sift once more. Rub or cut in ¼ cup of shortening with a stiff knife or pastry blender. Then stir in ⅔ cup of very cold milk. Work lightly into a smooth dough. Pat out about half an inch thick on a lightly floured board. Cut into rounds about 3 inches in diameter. Put on a baking sheet, and bake in a very hot oven (450 degrees F.) for 12 to 15 minutes. Quickly remove from the oven, and split in two.

Place a burger, broiled just at the moment, on each biscuit half, which has been brushed with prepared mustard to taste. Adjust the other biscuit halves. Press gently, and serve at once. Garnish with slices of dill pickle, placed on lettuce leaves, and a raw slice of tomato, topped with a puff of mayonnaise.

## BURGER SHORTCAKE II
*Serves 6*

Prepare biscuit dough, and cut it ¼ inch thick and 3 inches in diameter. Do not bake it. Place burgers on 6 unbaked biscuit halves, which have been spread with prepared mustard. Top with the other unbaked halves. Press the edges lightly together. Bake on a greased baking sheet in a very hot oven (450 degrees F.) about 20 minutes. Serve with tomato sauce, and garnish with watercress.

### BURGER SOUFFLÉ                                     (103)
*Serves 6*

Melt 2 tablespoons of butter. Blend in 2 tablespoons of flour
until smooth and the mixture bubbles, but do not let it brown.
Then stir in gradually 1 cup of undiluted evaporated milk, stirring
constantly until the mixture thickens, over a gentle flame. Stir in
½ cup of soft bread crumbs and ½ pound of lean raw ground beef,
keeping on stirring while adding, and seasoning with salt and pepper and a generous grating of nutmeg. Then stir in, one at a time,
2 unbeaten egg yolks, beating well after each addition. Cook for 1
minute longer, keeping on stirring. Remove from the fire. Cool a
little. Then fold in 3 egg whites, stiffly beaten. Turn the mixture
into a generously buttered soufflé dish, a glass one preferably. Place
in a pan containing hot, not boiling, water, and bake for 30 to 35
minutes in a moderate oven (350 degrees F.). Serve immediately.

*In 420 B.C., Alcibiades of Greece, who owned a silver service of a
thousand plates, was forced to borrow three hundred more from
the state treasury for his lavish parties.*

### BURGER SOUP                                        (104)
*French method—serves 6 generously*

A real one-meal dish.

Place 1 pound of beef bones, cut into 3 or 4 pieces, in a large
soup kettle. Cover with cold water, using 2 quarts. Bring to the
boiling point, lower the flame, and let simmer for 1¼ hours, without skimming. Then add 1 bunch of scallions, coarsely chopped
after being thoroughly cleaned in several cold waters, to the last of
which is added 1 tablespoon of vinegar, then thoroughly drained.
Add 5 medium-sized fresh tomatoes, peeled and quartered; 3 stalks
of celery, cut into small pieces; and 2 leeks, thoroughly washed and
cut into ½-inch pieces. Continue simmering for 30 minutes.

Meantime, heat 3 tablespoons of butter, and brown into it 1½
pounds of lean raw ground beef, stirring constantly with a fork to
separate the lumps, and cooking only until the meat begins to
change color. Add this to the soup with 4 medium-sized carrots,
grated, then quartered. Add also a bouquet garni composed of 1
large bay leaf tied with 4 sprigs of green celery tops, 6 sprigs of

parsley, and 1 sprig of thyme, or the equivalent of thyme leaves. Add 10 whole peppercorns, gently bruised, and 1 tablespoon of salt, more or less. Let this simmer, covered, for 45 minutes. Discard the soupbones, and serve the soup in hot plates, each garnished with a small round of toasted bread, topped with grated Gruyère cheese.

(105)

## BURGER IN SOUR CREAM
*Chinese method—serves 6*

Season 1½ pounds of lean raw ground beef to taste with salt, pepper, and 1 generous tablespoon of Worcestershire sauce, and form into 6 flat pancakes. Heat 3 tablespoons of cooking oil, and when hot, fry in it 1 medium-sized onion, thinly sliced, over a bright flame, stirring almost constantly until well browned. Add the cakes, and fry on both sides until brown, and pink pearls rise on top. Remove the cakes from the pan, leaving the onion slices, and arrange them on a hot platter. Mix well ¾ cup of rich sour cream, 1 scant teaspoon of prepared mustard, ⅔ teaspoon of soy sauce, a dash of paprika, and salt and pepper to taste. Pour over the onion slices in the pan. Allow to bubble several times, then strain this sauce over the burger pancakes. Garnish with watercress, and serve at once with a side dish of plain boiled rice.

*One of the richest men in Italy in the eighth century was a certain Rinaldo, the food man. He spent his working hours inventing new dishes and employed 300 scribes to write out the resulting recipes, which made a fortune for him.*

(106)

## BURGER SPAGHETTI CASSEROLE AU GRATIN
*Serves 6*

Heat ¼ cup of fat to the smoking point, then stir in 2 pounds of lean raw ground beef chuck, mixed with ¼ pound of lean raw ground pork and 2 medium-sized onions, grated. Cook until the burger begins to brown. Season with salt, pepper, 1 small clove of garlic, chopped fine, and ½ teaspoon of sage. Stir in 2 pounds of spaghetti cooked in boiling salted water and well drained. Blend well, adding while blending 2 tall cans of tomato juice. Turn all into a greased casserole. Cover tightly, and bake for 25 minutes.

Uncover. Sprinkle with ½ cup of buttered bread crumbs, mixed with ⅓ cup of grated American cheese. Let brown in the oven or under the flame of the broiling oven. Serve in the casserole.

(107)

## BURGER BALLS IN SPAGHETTI RING
*Serves 6*

Cook 1 package of spaghetti in boiling salted water until tender, but not too soft. Drain. Mix with 3 tablespoons of melted butter, then with 1 can of tomato pulp, well drained. Pack the spaghetti mixture into a buttered ring mold, and keep hot while preparing the burger balls.

Mix together 1 pound of lean raw ground beef chuck; ½ pound of lean raw ground pork; ½ pound of meat sausage; 2 tablespoons of grated onion; 2 tablespoons of green pepper, chopped fine; 2 teaspoons of salt; ½ teaspoon of black pepper; and ¼ teaspoon each of thyme and nutmeg. Blend well, and form into 18 small balls. Pan-fry the balls in ¼ generous cup of bacon drippings for 6 or 7 minutes, shaking the pan frequently to brown the burger balls evenly. Drain.

Unmold the spaghetti ring mold onto a hot round platter. Fill the center with burger balls, well drained. Pour over the balls 1½ cups of your favorite brown gravy. Dust with minced parsley, and serve at once.

(108)

## BURGER SPINACH BALLS DINNER
*Serves 6*

Cook 2 pounds of fresh spinach, carefully washed and drained, in its own drippings for 5 or 6 minutes, covered. Drain. Chop. Season to taste with salt and pepper. Fry 2 medium-sized onions, chopped, in ¼ cup of cooking oil with 1 clove of garlic, finely chopped, until brown, or about 6 or 7 minutes. Then stir in 1¾ pounds of lean raw ground beef chuck, cooking for 3 or 4 minutes, and stirring with a fork to break the lumps. Remove from the fire, and turn into a mixing bowl. Then add ¼ generous cup of grated American cheese, 2 whole fresh eggs, slightly beaten, 2 teaspoons of salt, ½ teaspoon of pepper, 1 tablespoon each of chili sauce and Worcestershire sauce, and lastly the chopped spinach. Divide the mixture into 6 equal parts. Flatten a little, and pan-fry in ½ cup of bacon drippings on both sides for 10 minutes. Then pour over 1 cup of tomato sauce. Heat well, and pour the mixture into a ring of mashed potatoes, sprinkled with grated cheese and delicately browned under the flame of the broiling oven. Dust the burger balls and gravy with chopped parsley, and serve at once.

*In seventeenth-century Ireland, colds and similar ailments were treated by feeding the patient liquidized pork fat, while raw fish eggs were prescribed for lumbago and toothache.*

(109)

## BURGER STEAK WITH SOUBISE SAUCE
*Serves 6*

Mix together 2 pounds of lean raw ground beef chuck, 1 tablespoon of Worcestershire sauce, 2 tablespoons of grated onions, 2 tablespoons of chopped parsley, ½ teaspoon of sage, ¼ teaspoon of nutmeg, and 2 whole fresh eggs, slightly beaten. Divide the mixture into 6 equal parts, and shape into boats. Dip in melted butter, seasoned with a little lemon juice, celery salt to taste, and a few grains of cayenne pepper. Broil for 6 minutes on each side, or until little pinkish pearls appear on the surface. Keep hot.

*Soubise Sauce—Quick Method.* Cook until firm, but not mushy, 1½ cups of sliced onions in boiling water to cover. Drain, and reserve the water. Press the onions through a fine sieve. Melt ¼ scant cup of butter, add 3 tablespoons of flour, and blend well. When the mixture begins to bubble, stir in 1 cup of the onion water, ½ generous cup of scalded undiluted evaporated milk, salt and pepper to taste, and a grating of nutmeg, stirring constantly until smooth and creamy. Add the onion pulp, and reheat, adding additional seasoning if needed. Arrange the burger steaks on a hot platter. Surround with the onion sauce, dust with paprika, and serve at once.

(110)

## BURGER STEW I
*Home method—serves 6*

Mix together 1¼ pounds of lean raw ground beef chuck, ¾ pound of lean raw ground beef flank, 2 teaspoons of celery salt, 1 teaspoon of chili powder, 2 tablespoons of minced parsley, 2 tablespoons of grated onion, ½ scant cup of fine dry bread crumbs, no pepper at all, and 2 whole fresh eggs, slightly beaten. Mix well, and shape into small round balls with the floured palms of the hands, but *do not press* them too closely.

Put 1 quart of meat stock, made from leftover bones or from a small soupbone, in a wide shallow saucepan. Add ½ cup of sliced carrots; 1 medium-sized onion, thinly sliced; ½ green pepper, shredded and free from seeds and white ribs; 1 leek, cut into inch pieces, after being thoroughly washed; 1 large bay leaf tied with 4 or 5 sprigs of fresh parsley and 3 sprigs of green celery tops; and 1 whole clove. Heat to the boiling point. Let this simmer for 35 to 40 minutes. Then drop in the burger balls, after bringing the mixture to the boiling point. Cover, and let simmer gently until the vegetables are tender. If the stew boils too hard or fast, the burger balls will fall apart. Skim out the meat balls, and arrange them in the center of a hot platter. Thicken the gravy with 1 tablespoon of butter kneaded with 1 tablespoon of flour. Taste for seasoning, adding if needed. Let gently boil for 3 or 4 minutes. Pour the gravy and vegetables over the burger balls, and serve at once with a side dish of plain boiled potatoes.

*Between 1601 and 1640, French women were obsessed with the idea of being petite. They tried to achieve it by eating several duck eggs daily, but to no avail.*

(111)

### BURGER STEW II
*Home method—serves 6*

Mix together 1 pound of lean raw ground beef flank, ½ pound of lean raw ground veal, ½ pound of meat sausage, 1 rounded tablespoon of uncooked rice, 2 whole fresh eggs, slightly beaten, 2 teaspoons of salt, ½ teaspoon of black pepper, ½ teaspoon of sage, ¼ teaspoon of clove, and 1 teaspoon of Worcestershire sauce. Form into 18 balls without pressing, lest the balls when cooked are tough. Place a No. 2 can of tomatoes in a heavy saucepan, and let simmer to sauce consistency. Then add the burger balls; 1 dozen peeled small white onions; 1 dozen small canned mushrooms; 3 stalks of celery, grated, then cut into ½-inch pieces; 2 whole cloves; 1 large bay leaf tied with 6 sprigs of fresh parsley; and ½ teaspoon of Worcestershire sauce. Cover tightly, and set in a moderate oven (350 degrees F.) for 1¼ hours, without disturbing. Look once to see if there is need of more liquid, if so, add it. Serve in a hot deep platter with plain boiled potatoes.

(112)

## BURGER STUFFED GREEN PEPPER
*Serves 6*

Select 6 medium-sized green peppers of uniform size. Wash them, cut a slice from the stem ends, and remove the seeds, leaving the white ribs. Drop them into boiling water, and let simmer gently for 4 or 5 minutes. Remove from the water, and drain. Set aside. Heat ¼ cup of shortening to the smoking point. Add 1½ pounds of lean raw ground beef flank or chuck, seasoned to taste with about 1½ teaspoons of salt, or celery salt, if preferred, and ½ scant teaspoon of black pepper; 2 cups of drained cooked rice; 1 tablespoon of grated onion; and 1 tablespoon of chopped parsley. Cook and stir about 10 minutes. Remove from the fire, and stir in ½ generous cup of chopped ripe olives. Blend thoroughly. Stand the green peppers on end in a baking dish, and fill with the stuffing mixture. Sprinkle the tops with grated American cheese, using about ½ generous cup. Adjust the slices that were cut from the stem ends. Pour over them 1 cup of meat stock, broth, hot water mixed with 2 bouillon cubes, tomato juice, tomato soup, mushroom soup, or any other kind of soup or juice. Bake for 35 to 40 minutes in a slow oven (325 degrees F.), or until the pepper shells are tender and slightly blistered. Serve hot with French fried potatoes.

(113)

## BURGER STUFFED ONIONS
*Serves 6*

Select 6 extra large onions or 12 small ones. The 8-ounce Bermuda onions are fine for the large ones. Peel carefully, removing the tough peeling as far as possible. Cover the peeled onions with boiling salted water, and cook until nearly tender, or about 15 to 20 minutes, the time depending on the size of the onions. Drain and cool. You may use the filling indicated for the above recipe, or the following mixture.

Cut a slice from the top of each onion, and carefully scoop out the center, leaving an outside shell a scant inch thick. Chop the pulp coarsely. Sauté ½ cup of fresh or canned sliced mushrooms in ¼ cup of butter with the onion pulp about 5 minutes. Then stir in 1 pound of lean raw ground beef chuck; salt and pepper to taste; 1 tablespoon of chopped parsley; 1 teaspoon of Worcestershire sauce; 1 pinch each of mace, clove, and thyme leaves; ¼ cup of soft bread crumbs; and 1 whole fresh egg. Mix well. Fill the onion shells with the mixture. Cover with buttered bread crumbs mixed in equal parts with grated cheese. Place the stuffed onions in a pan containing 1 cup of tomato juice, meat stock, canned bouillon, or water. Bake for 35 minutes in a moderate oven (350 degrees F.), basting frequently with the liquid in the pan. Serve hot with buttered noodles, if desired.

*Eighteenth-century etiquette required a polished gentleman to tie a napkin around a lady's neck when they dined together. Neglecting to do so was exceedingly bad manners.*

(114)

## BURGER STUFFED TOMATOES
### Serves 6

On an unpretentious old frame house in Newport, Rhode Island, the historical society of that community has placed an equally plain marker, with the legend: "Corne House; Home of the Artist, Michele Felice Corné, who Introduced the Tomato into this Country." If you belong to the cult that takes its morning tomato juice as a rite and the fruit itself as one of the first articles of diet, salute Michele Corné. He was its apostle and its prophet. And he invented spicy tomato sauce.

Wash 6 large tomatoes, but do not peel. Remove the stem ends, and scoop out some of the pulp with a teaspoon. Turn the tomatoes upside down to drain. Then sprinkle the tomato cups with mixed salt and pepper, and stuff lightly with the following mixture.

Mix the pulp of tomatoes with ¾ pound of lean raw ground beef chuck; 1 tablespoon each of grated onion and parsley, the latter finely chopped; a tiny bit of garlic to taste; 1 teaspoon of Worcestershire sauce; salt and pepper to taste; and a dash each of thyme and clove. Fill the tomato cups lightly to the brim. Top each with buttered bread crumbs mixed with grated cheese, ½ generous cup for all. Place in a greased baking dish, and bake in a moderate oven (350 degrees F.) for 30 minutes, or until tender, the time depending on the size of the tomatoes. Serve very hot.

*In 1645, the Persian government passed a law whereby astrologers could be paid only in food. A large sum of gold might tempt them to dishonesty, but a large amount of food would only go bad.*

BURGER STUFFED WHOLE CABBAGE
*Serves 6*

In Wisconsin, they have a way of preparing a delicious dish out of the delicious vegetable called cabbage, to treat oneself to which it is not necessary to be a millionaire. This is the recipe.

When your cabbage, a beautiful green cabbage it must be, and 2½ pounds if you please, is half cooked (parboiled whole in a large kettle, head down), lift it out of the kettle, and set it in a colander to drain, placing it upside down. Then take it out, and set it on a clean board. Unfold it gently, very gently, pushing leaf by leaf without tearing, exactly as you might open a rose. Now it is a cupola, a rose design, the work of an expert architect.

In a platter have waiting this delicious stuffing made of ½ pound of meat sausage; ¾ pound of lean raw ground beef chuck or plate; 2 slices of bread, soaked in cold milk, then squeezed through a clean cloth; all expertly seasoned with thyme leaves, powdered cloves, 1 tablespoon of chopped parsley, 1 tablespoon of grated onion, a taste of garlic, 1 tablespoon of Worcestershire sauce, and 1 teaspoon of prepared mustard; 2 whole eggs, fresh and slightly beaten; and salt and black pepper to taste. A fine stuffing indeed!

Then with care, with gentleness, with an artist's patience, spread this stuffing on each leaf with a spatula, and evenly. When all the leaves have received their share of this soft and highly perfumed paste, with a lightly caressing hand, bring back the leaves and press them gently all around the heart of the cabbage, which has received its share of the stuffing in the shape of a ball. The dome reappears. The cabbage is again in shape as it came from the garden, as if nothing had happened.

Tie it elegantly, and set it softly in a generously buttered fireproof earthenware baking dish, containing a No. 2 can of tomatoes, liquid and pulp, mixed with a little roux. Stick it then with 3 whole cloves, and let the dish slide gently into a moderately hot oven (325 degrees F.), where it will slowly, rhythmically cook and develop an aroma to remember. When ready to serve, sprinkle over it 1 or 2 tablespoons of capers. Do not forget to add to the already fine sauce 1 generous tablespoon of good sherry, or 1 pony glass of good brandy. The cabbage loves it just as much as you do. The cabbage is now ready for the table, where a subdued excitement ushers in the ceremonial serving and tasting of this exceptional dish. (See No. 157 for roux.)

## BURGER TAMALE PIE I (116)
### Serves 6

For a luncheon alfresco on a torrid August afternoon, or a supper before a roaring fire of logs on February's most blustery night, prepare a tamale pie thus.

Prepare a mush by stirring 1 cup of corn meal with ¾ teaspoon of salt into 3 cups of boiling water, meat stock, or canned bouillon. Cook, stirring almost constantly, for 15 minutes. Brown lightly 2 tablespoons of chopped onion and 1 clove of garlic, finely chopped, in 1 generous tablespoon of bacon drippings. Then add 1 pound of lean raw ground beef chuck or plate, and cook for 2 minutes only, stirring with a fork to break the lumps, if any. Season with ½ generous teaspoon of salt, 1 generous teaspoon of chili pepper (more or less according to taste), 1 generous tablespoon of minced canned pimientos, and 1 generous cup of thick seasoned tomato purée. Grease a baking dish, and line the dish with the mush. Add the burger mixture, and cover with the remainder of the mush. Brush over with melted bacon drippings. Bake in a moderate oven (350 degrees F.) for 30 minutes or so. Serve in the baking dish.

*Polite New Yorkers, when dining in restaurants in the 1870's, tucked one napkin under their chins, and spread another over their laps.*

## BURGER TAMALE PIE II (117)
### Southwestern method—serves 6 generously

Bring to a boil 3 cups of water with 1 teaspoon of salt, and slowly stir in 1 cup of corn meal. Cook for 15 to 20 minutes. Then add 1 cup of ripe olives, stoned and cut into pieces. Set aside to cool. Melt 2 generous tablespoons of fat, and add 1 large onion and 1 large green pepper, both finely chopped. Cook for 2 minutes, stirring frequently. Then stir in 1½ pounds of lean raw ground beef chuck or plate, mixing thoroughly with a fork to break lumps, if any. Cook until the burger begins to brown. Then add 2 cups of canned tomatoes, pulp and liquid, 1 teaspoon of chili powder (more if desired very hot and peppery), and ¾ teaspoon of salt. Cook gently for 10 minutes. Put half the corn meal mush in a generously greased casserole. Add the cooked burger mixture, and cover with the remaining mush. Brush the top with bacon fat, and bake in a moderate oven (350 degrees F.) for 30 minutes. Serve sizzling hot.

(118)

## BURGER À LA TARTARE
*Individual serving*

Spread over 1 buttered slice of bread, toasted or not, ⅓ pound of lean raw ground beef chuck or plate, mixed with 1 teaspoon of grated onion, having the edge a little higher than the center. Or make a depression in the center, and in it put 1 fresh egg yolk. Sprinkle the whole with mixed salt and pepper to taste, the egg yolk with minced parsley or chives, and serve at once.

(119)

## BURGER TOMATO LUNCHEON
*Serves 6*

Cut 3 large tomatoes in half crosswise. Take off a slice from the uncut sides. Season with salt and pepper, sprinkle with melted butter, and broil or fry in a pan in fat until delicately browned. Place each on a round of toast, the size of the tomato slice, and top each tomato slice with a burger cake prepared as follows.

Mix 1¾ pounds of lean raw ground beef, 2 whole fresh eggs, ½ cup of soft bread crumbs, 1¾ teaspoons of salt, ½ teaspoon of pepper, 2 tablespoons of grated onion, and 1 tablespoon of chopped parsley. Divide the mixture into 6 equal portions, and shape into cakes. Roll in melted butter seasoned with a few dashes of Tabasco and Worcestershire sauce. Pan-fry in ¼ cup of fat, allowing 5 minutes on each side. Top each burger with 2 slices of broiled bacon. Garnish the platter with watercress and ripe olives, and serve at once.

During the twelfth century in Sicily, the up-to-date noble was always accompanied by his individual chef, who was generally a dwarf.

BURGER TOMATO TART                                        (120)
*Serves 6*

Cut 4 tomatoes in thick slices without peeling. Sprinkle with mixed salt, freshly ground black pepper, and a few grains of curry powder to taste. Dredge in corn meal. Fry very slowly in hot bacon drippings, using about ¼ generous cup, so that the slices will be well cooked. Sprinkle a little sugar on each slice after frying. Line a 9-inch pie plate or tin with rich pie dough. Arrange the tomato slices around the edge, and in the center place 12 small balls of burger, the size of a walnut, prepared as follows.

Mix ¾ pound of lean raw ground beef chuck, ½ pound of meat sausage, 1 scant tablespoon of grated onion, 1 scant tablespoon of chopped parsley, 1 whole fresh egg, 1 teaspoon of Worcestershire sauce, and salt and pepper to taste. (You may add a little crushed garlic to the meat mixture, if desired.) Mix well, divide into 12 parts, and shape into balls. Adjust the top crust over the tomato slices and burgers after pouring over them ½ scant cup of your favorite brown gravy. Slash the top for escape of steam. Brush it with milk, egg yolk, or butter. Bake for 10 long minutes in a very hot oven (450 degrees F.). Reduce the temperature to moderate (350 degrees F.), and continue baking for 15 to 20 minutes longer. Serve very hot.

BURGER TURNOVERS                                          (121)
*Makes 6*

Mix together very lightly 1¼ pounds of lean raw ground beef; 2 teaspoons of grated onion; 2 teaspoons of chopped parsley; salt, pepper, and nutmeg to taste; and 2 tablespoons of rich tomato sauce. Set aside while making your favorite pie dough, which roll out in a sheet not more than ⅛ inch thick. Cut in 6 oblongs 2 by 4 inches, or in squares 3 by 3. Place 1 generous tablespoon of burger mixture on half of each oblong or square, and moisten the edges of the dough with cold water. Fold the other half over the meat mixture, and pinch the edges firmly together. Prick twice on top with a fork. Place the turnovers on a greased baking sheet, and bake in a hot oven (400–425 degrees F.) for 18 to 20 minutes. Serve with your favorite creamed green vegetable and a few French or home fried potatoes.

(122)

## BURGER UPSIDE-DOWN PIE
*Serves 6*

In a 9-inch skillet, cook 3 tablespoons of finely chopped onion in 3 generous tablespoons of fat, for 2 or 3 minutes. Stir in 1 generous pound of lean raw ground beef chuck, and cook, stirring with a fork to break up the lumps, until the meat is lightly browned. Then add 1 can of cream of tomato soup, or of tomato purée. Mix thoroughly, then season with salt, pepper, nutmeg, and sage to taste. Spread the top with savory biscuit dough.

*Savory Biscuit Dough.* Mix 1½ cups of bread flour, which has been sifted once and then measured, with 1½ teaspoons of baking powder, ½ generous teaspoon of salt, ¼ teaspoon of pepper, 1½ teaspoons of paprika, and 1 teaspoon of celery salt. Then sift twice into a mixing bowl. Work in 5 tablespoons of lard or other shortening to the consistency of meal, then stir in ¾ scant cup of very cold sweet milk. Beat for ½ minute, then pat out on a lightly floured board to a round, 9 inches in diameter and ¼ scant inch thick. Adjust over the meat mixture, brush with cold milk, and bake in a hot oven (425 degrees F.) about 15 minutes. Turn upside down on a hot platter. Garnish with parsley, ripe olives rolled in hot bacon fat, then in sieved bread crumbs, and broiled slices of green or ripe tomatoes.

*In the days of Emperor Charlemagne, in France and Germany, the ladies used to rise from the table when men approached and sit down only after the gentlemen were seated. Today it's the opposite.*

(123)

## BURGER TOMATO CHEESE SOUFFLÉ
*Serves 6*

Never plan a soufflé for a dinner that may be delayed, as it must be served hot from the oven. Right combination is the secret of a good soufflé.

Combine 3 tablespoons of quick-cooking tapioca, 1 teaspoon of salt, and 1 cup of tomato soup in the top of a double boiler. Place over rapidly boiling water, and cook for 8 to 10 minutes after the water boils again, stirring frequently. Add ½ cup of grated American cheese and ½ pound of lean raw ground beef chuck or plate. Stir until the cheese is melted and the meat has changed color. Cool slightly. Beat in 3 egg yolks, already slightly beaten, then fold in 3 egg whites, stiffly beaten. Turn into a greased soufflé dish. Place in a pan of hot water, and bake in a moderate oven (350 degrees F.) for 15 to 20 minutes, or until the soufflé is puffed and firm. Serve immediately.

*Note.* You may bake 6 individual soufflés in buttered ramekins, if desired, at the same temperature but a little longer, or about 25 minutes.

## BURGER WAFFLES (124)
*Southern method—serves 6*

Mix and sift together 3 cups of sifted cake flour, 2 tablespoons of baking powder, 1 generous pinch of powdered cloves, and 1 tiny pinch of dry mustard into a mixing bowl. In another mixing bowl, combine 3 whole fresh eggs, well beaten; 1 teaspoon of brown sugar; ¾ pound of twice-ground lean raw beef chuck; 2¼ cups of sweet cold milk; and ½ generous cup of melted butter. Mix thoroughly and combine with the flour mixture, then beat until smooth. Bake for 4 to 5 minutes in a hot waffle iron, sprinkling 1 tablespoon of finely minced bacon over each waffle before closing the iron. Serve very hot with a side dish of your favorite brown sauce or gravy, or with leftover gravy from the roast.

## CHINESE BURGER PLATE (125)
*Serves 6*

Combine and mix thoroughly, then put through a food chopper, 1¾ pounds of lean raw ground beef chuck; 1 dozen chopped water chestnuts; salt and pepper; 1 pinch of powdered ginger mixed with ½ teaspoon of baking powder; and 1 generous teaspoon of peanut oil mixed with 2 tablespoons of Chinese sauce. (A pinch of baking powder, Chinese chefs will tell you, does wonders in loosening the fibers of tough meat.) Shape into a large pancake, and pan-fry in 3 tablespoons of peanut oil, until brown on both sides, but not too well done inside. Turn onto a hot platter, and serve with boiled rice and Chinese brown sauce.

*Chinese Proverb: Though breakfast be good, dinner is better.*

(126)

COTTAGE BURGER PIE
  *Serves 6*

Place 1½ pounds of lean raw ground beef and ½ pound of meat sausage, ground together, in a frying pan containing 3 tablespoons of bacon drippings. Brown lightly, stirring with a fork to break the lumps, if any. In another frying pan, heat 2 tablespoons of bacon drippings, and fry in it ¼ cup of chopped celery, 2 tablespoons of chopped onion, and 1 tablespoon of chopped green pepper, for 2 minutes, stirring constantly. Then add the meat mixture; ½ cup of washed, drained, and sponged seedless raisins; 3 hard-cooked eggs, chopped; and ½ cup of ripe olives, sliced. Stir in 2 cups of your favorite brown gravy. Mix thoroughly, and turn into a deep pie dish. Cover with rich biscuit dough. Bake for 15 to 20 minutes, or until the top is delicately browned, in a very hot oven (425 degrees F.). Serve very hot.

(127)

CREAMED BURGER ON TOAST
  *Army method—serves 6*

Prepare 2 cups of medium white sauce as indicated in recipe No. 90. Keep hot. Heat 2 tablespoons of bacon drippings or lard, and slightly brown in it 2 pounds of lean raw ground beef, seasoned with 1½ teaspoons of salt, 2 tablespoons of grated onion, and ½ teaspoon of white pepper, as well as a generous grating of nutmeg. Stir with a fork to break any lumps. Drain off the fat thoroughly, and add the meat to the white sauce. Blend well, and serve on freshly made buttered toast, after dusting with minced parsley.

(128)

CUBAN BURGER PIE
  *Serves 6 generously*

Pare 6 medium-sized potatoes, and slice into a greased baking dish. Season to taste with salt, pepper, and a little curry powder, and add 1 medium-sized onion, chopped. Then cover with milk, and bake.

Meantime, mix together 2 pounds of lean raw ground beef chuck or plate; salt, pepper, and nutmeg to taste; 1 clove of garlic, finely chopped; 2 tablespoons of grated onion; ½ cup of cold milk; and 2 whole fresh eggs, slightly beaten with 3 tablespoons of grated American cheese. Mix well, and shape into 12 small balls. Fry in hot deep fat until brown, but soft inside.

When the potatoes are almost done, remove them from the oven. Sprinkle with 1 cup of grated American cheese. Then lay the burger balls over the potatoes, and return to the oven to bake about 15 minutes.

Meantime, prepare enough baking powder biscuits to cover the top of the burger balls. Then put back in a hot oven (425 degrees F.) for 15 to 18 minutes, or until the biscuits are done and brown. Serve at once.

(129)

### ENGLISH BURGER PIE
*Serves 6*

Mix 2 pounds of lean raw ground beef chuck with salt, pepper, and nutmeg to taste, and add 2 tablespoons each of grated onion and minced parsley. Blend well. Spread a layer of this in a greased baking dish. Sprinkle with ¼ generous cup of buttered bread crumbs. Repeat the layers until the dish is nearly full, seasoning each layer with a few drops of Worcestershire sauce. Pour over all 1 cup of meat stock, leftover meat gravy, or hot water with a little butter melted in it. Sprinkle on the top a good layer of buttered bread crumbs. Cover tightly, and bake for 30 minutes in a moderate oven (375 degrees F.). Remove the cover, and brown well. Serve very hot.

*In aristocratic sixteenth-century Irish homes, the hands of the diners were washed and dried between each course by two pages especially assigned to that occupation.*

(130)

### ENGLISH BURGER SAVORY PUDDING
*Serves 6*

Heat ¼ cup of butter or margarine, and add 1 cup of chopped onions. Fry until they begin to turn yellow, stirring constantly, then stir in ½ teaspoon of granulated sugar. Set aside. Add 1½ teaspoons of salt, ¼ teaspoon of pepper, and 1 generous pinch each of sage, thyme, marjoram, and summer savory to a No. 2 can of tomatoes, and blend well. Put a layer of the tomato mixture in the bottom of a greased baking dish. Sprinkle with some of the fried onion. Then place a layer of lean raw ground beef, using about 1½ pounds of beef altogether. Repeat in this way until all is used. Sprinkle the top with ⅓ cup of small bread cubes, then with ½ scant cup of grated cheese. Cover and bake for 30 minutes in a moderately hot oven (350 degrees F.). Then uncover, and bake for 15 minutes longer to brown. Serve at once.

(131)

### FINNISH BURGER BALLS
*Serves 6*

Mix lightly 2 pounds of lean raw ground beef; ¼ cup of chopped onion, browned in 1½ tablespoons of butter, using both butter and onion; 1 cup of soft bread crumbs; ½ cup of milk; 2 whole fresh eggs, well beaten; and salt, pepper, and thyme to taste. Shape into 18 small balls. Pan-fry in ¼ cup of butter (Finns never use oil or lard) until brown all over. Serve on a hot platter covered with a mound of fluffy mashed potatoes, mixed with well-browned onion rings.

(132)

### FLEMISH BURGER ROLL
*Mock rabbit—serves 6*

Mix very lightly 2 pounds of lean raw ground beef chuck; ¾ cup of bread crumbs; 2 tablespoons of grated onion; salt and pepper to taste; 1 tablespoon of chopped chives; and 1 generous pinch each of thyme, cinnamon, nutmeg, sage, and chopped tarragon herb. Beat very lightly 2 whole fresh eggs with ½ generous cup of rich meat stock or bouillon, and add to the mixture, which should be rather soft. Let stand overnight in the refrigerator. Next day, roll into a large sausage. Place in a generously buttered fireproof dish. Cover entire top with thinly sliced raw onions, then with a buttered paper. Bake in a moderate oven (350 degrees F.) for 1 hour. Remove the paper, and let brown for about 12 to 15 minutes. Serve hot or cold.

According to law in seventeenth-century Corsica, a man might divorce his wife by ejecting her from his house. But for the rest of her life, he was compelled to send her food daily.

(133)

### HAITIAN BURGER SURPRISE
*Serves 6*

Mix lightly 1¾ pounds of lean raw ground beef chuck or plate; 1¼ teaspoons of salt; ¼ teaspoon of black pepper, freshly ground; ¼ teaspoon each of thyme, sage, allspice, and marjoram; 1 generous teaspoon each of grated onion and finely minced parsley; and ½ teaspoon of grated lemon rind. Bind with 2 whole fresh eggs, slightly beaten with ¼ scant cup of milk, and ½ cup of soft bread crumbs. Divide the burger mixture into 6 equal parts, and shape into sausages. Place in each center a piece of banana dipped in lemon juice, and fasten a slice of bacon around the edge with a toothpick. Broil for 5 minutes on each side, or longer if desired medium or well done. Serve the burgers on a hot platter with a side dish of rich tomato sauce.

(134)

### HUNGARIAN BURGER BALLS
*Serves 6*

Put in a saucepan 1½ cups of meat stock, canned bouillon, or water; 2 tablespoons of finely chopped onion; a bouquet garni composed of 1 large bay leaf, 5 or 6 sprigs of fresh parsley, 2 sprigs of green celery tops, and 1 small branch of thyme, tied together with white thread; salt to taste; 6 whole peppercorns, crushed; and ½ scant teaspoon of allspice. Bring to a boil, reduce the heat, and let simmer for 20 minutes. Strain, and keep hot.

Mix together ¾ pound of lean raw ground beef chuck; ¾ pound of lean raw ground pork; 1 tablespoon of grated onion; ¼ cup of soft bread crumbs; salt and pepper to taste; and 3 egg whites, stiffly beaten. After mixing well, shape into 12 balls, pressing very lightly, but thoroughly.

Bring the first mixture to the boiling point, and drop the balls into it. Allow to boil for 15 minutes, but not too briskly. Skim the balls with a skimmer, and keep them hot. To the strained remaining stock, in which the burger balls were boiled, add a grating of nutmeg, ½ generous teaspoon of prepared mustard, and 3 table-spoons of tarragon vinegar. Bring to a boil, then stir in 1 tablespoon of butter kneaded with 1 scant tablespoon of flour. Let boil for 5 minutes. When smooth, strain through a fine sieve. Then beat in 3 egg yolks, one at a time, beating briskly after each addition. Place the pan over hot water, and let simmer for 3 or 4 minutes, or just enough to cook the egg yolks, stirring constantly to prevent curdling.

Strain this sauce over the burger balls, and dust with mixed paprika and chopped parsley. Garnish with 1 dozen small triangles of bread, fried in butter. Serve at once with a side dish of Parisienne potatoes.

*Parisienne Potatoes.* Cut enough potatoes, as required, with a Parisienne cutter, that is, into small balls. Blanch in boiling salted water. Drain thoroughly, then pan-fry in plenty of butter until a light brown color has been achieved. Drain again. Sprinkle slightly with salt and a little white pepper, then with parsley.

*Chinese chefs of the seventeenth century were graded among themselves according to the number and kind of recipes they knew, and a southern chef was not eligible for employment in the north.*

(135)

## HUNTER'S BURGER DINNER
*Serves 6*

In an iron pan, put 3 slices of bacon, diced small, and fry, stirring often, over a gentle fire, until the bacon begins to crisp. Then add 4 medium-sized onions and 1 generous clove of garlic, both chopped very fine. Continue frying and stirring until the onion is getting brown. Now add 2 pounds of lean raw ground beef, mixed with ¼ pound of lean raw ground pork or veal, and 2 tablespoons of parsley, chopped very fine. Season to taste with salt and pepper, and add ¼ teaspoon each of clove, thyme, and sage. Stir almost constantly, until the mixture is well separated. Lower the flame as low as possible. Let simmer for 35 to 40 minutes, or until the mixture is just moist, but with no great amount of its own liquid in the pan. Serve at once with a green vegetable, plain boiled potatoes, and a fruit for dessert.

(136)

## INDIVIDUAL BURGER PIES
*Makes 6*

Heat 2 tablespoons of fat. Add 3 medium-sized onions, thinly sliced, and fry until the onions are beginning to brown, stirring frequently. Then stir in 1¼ pounds of lean raw ground beef chuck or plate, and cook until the meat is brown, stirring very frequently to blend well and separate lumps, if any. Then add 4 medium-sized peeled and diced small potatoes; salt and pepper to taste; 1 generous pinch of basil; ¼ teaspoon of thyme; ⅓ teaspoon of sage; 2 cups of canned tomatoes, pulp and liquid; and 1 cup of drained canned peas. Cover, and cook until the potatoes are almost done. Transfer to 6 generously greased individual baking dishes. Cover the tops with biscuit dough. Bake in a very hot oven (450 degrees F.) for 12 minutes, or until the crust is baked to a delicate brown. Serve immediately.

(137)

## INDIVIDUAL BURGER TARTLETS
*Makes 6*

Mix together 1 pound of lean raw ground beef chuck or plate; ½ pound of lean raw ground veal; 2 tablespoons of green pepper, finely chopped; 2 whole fresh eggs, slightly beaten; 2 tablespoons of grated onion; salt and pepper to taste; and ¼ teaspoon of thyme. Then stir in ¼ cup of tomato soup. Have some pastry dough ready. Roll out ⅛ inch thick on a lightly floured board. Cut into 6 rounds to fit 6 large muffin sections. After filling each, fold the edges of the dough over the mixture, having moistened the edge with water. Press with the tines of a fork. Brush with milk, and prick the centers with a fork for escape of steam. Bake for 10 minutes in a very hot oven (450 degrees F.). Then reduce the temperature to 400 degrees F., and continue baking for 20 minutes longer. Serve hot.

(138)

## ITALIAN BURGER SHORTCAKE
*Serves 6*

Have ready a baking powder biscuit dough. Divide into 2 equal portions, and roll each portion to fit a 9-inch round or square pan. Spread generously with melted butter. Adjust the second portion on top of the first, and bake for 20 minutes in a hot oven (400 degrees F.). While hot, separate the two parts, and put the following burger filling between the layers and on top.

Heat 4 tablespoons of cooking oil to the smoking point. Add 2 tablespoons of minced onion and 1 large clove of garlic, finely chopped. Cook until the onion is beginning to brown, turning frequently. Then stir in 1½ pounds of lean raw ground beef chuck, mixed with 1 small green pepper, chopped fine, salt and pepper to taste, and ¼ teaspoon each of thyme, basil, and nutmeg. Cook for 2 or 3 minutes, stirring constantly. Then pour over gradually 2 cups of hot meat stock or canned bouillon, stirring constantly. Cover, and allow to simmer very gently for 15 minutes. Ladle the mixture between the layers, reserving some for the top. Serve at once.

*Physicians of Ancient Rome frequently prescribed the following as a household cure-all: "Pound with care two walnuts, two dried figs, twenty pounds (?) rice, and a grain of salt." Which may be where the adage to "take with a grain of salt" originated.*

(139)

## JUICY BURGER BALLS
*Serves 6*

Mix lightly 1¾ pounds of lean raw ground beef chuck or plate; salt and pepper to taste; ¼ cup of heavy sour cream; ½ cup of soft bread crumbs; 3 whole eggs, slightly beaten; 2 tablespoons of grated onion; and 2 tablespoons of chopped parsley. Chill thoroughly. When ready to serve, remove from the refrigerator, and shape into 12 balls, flattened slightly. Cook for 3 to 4 minutes on each side on a greased griddle, uncovered. Serve dressed on cooked branch spinach, generously buttered.

(140)

## MEXICAN BURGER BALLS
*Serves 6*

Chop very fine—do not grind—2 pounds of lean raw beef chuck or plate. Mix lightly with 2 generous tablespoons of cooking oil, 1 generous pinch each of saffron and nutmeg, ¼ generous teaspoon of allspice, and salt and black pepper to taste. Then mix in 2 whole fresh eggs, slightly beaten with 2 tablespoons of tomato catsup. Shape into 12 balls. Set aside. Put 2 pounds of onions, thinly sliced, in a saucepan. Pour over enough rich meat stock or canned bouillon to cover. Add 1 scant teaspoon of powdered cinnamon. Cook until the onions are tender. Salt to taste. Add ½ generous teaspoon of chili sauce. Arrange the meat balls in a fireproof dish. Pour the onion and liquid over the balls. Bake for 25 to 30 minutes in a moderate oven (350 degrees F.). Serve very hot with a side dish of plain boiled potatoes.

(141)

### PAN-BROILED SCRAPED BURGERS
Serves 6

Wipe 2 pounds of lean raw beef chuck with a damp cloth, and scrape the meat with the back of a knife until shredded. Season with salt and pepper to taste and 1 tablespoon of grated onion. Shape into 12 flat cakes. Lightly pan-broil on an ungreased hot frying pan. Serve on freshly made buttered toast.

(142)

### RUMANIAN SAUSAGE
Carnatzei—serves 6

Combine 1¾ pounds of twice-ground lean raw beef; 1 clove of garlic, finely chopped; 1 teaspoon of paprika; 1½ teaspoons of salt; and ½ scant cup of cold canned bouillon or strained meat stock. Mix lightly, and shape into sausage forms. Broil for 4 to 5 minutes on each side, rolling them to insure even cooking. Serve with a side dish of French fried potatoes.

*At Grecian feasts in 95 B.C., the women were served bird meat. Male guests had to be content with mutton or pork.*

(143)

### SCALLOPED BURGER BALLS COUNTRY METHOD
Serves 6

Season 2 pounds of coarsely ground lean raw beef chuck with salt and pepper to taste and 2 tablespoons of onion juice. Add 2 whole fresh eggs, slightly beaten, and shape into 12 balls. Fry on both sides in ¼ cup of bacon drippings. Cover the bottom of a generously greased casserole (using the bacon drippings) with a layer of peeled and thinly sliced raw potatoes. Sprinkle with salt and pepper to taste and 1 pinch each of thyme, sage, and clove. Cover with meat balls, then with 2 large onions, peeled and thinly sliced. Dot with 2 tablespoons of butter, dotting the onions here and there. Pour over enough hot meat stock, canned bouillon, or water to come within an inch of the top of the casserole. Sprinkle over ½ cup of buttered soft bread crumbs. Cover with a buttered paper. Bake for 45 minutes in a moderate oven (350 degrees F.). Remove the paper, and continue baking for 10 minutes longer, or until the crumbs are delicately browned. Serve in the casserole.

(144)

## STEAMED BURGER TIMBALES
*Serves 6*

Boil together 2 tablespoons of butter with 4½ tablespoons of flour and 1 pinch of salt to taste in 1 cup of meat stock, stirring almost constantly, until the mixture is thick, or about 5 minutes. Cool, then combine with 1 pound of lean raw ground beef chuck, 2 whole fresh eggs, slightly beaten, 3 tablespoons of grated onion, 2 tablespoons of chopped parsley, and salt and pepper to taste. Butter 6 individual molds. Sprinkle in each 1 generous teaspoon of peeled and finely chopped raw mushrooms, using the stems and caps. Fill with the burger mixture. Place the molds in a pan containing hot water up to two-thirds of the molds. Set in a moderate oven (350 degrees F.) for 20 minutes. Serve hot with your favorite mushroom sauce and a side dish of mashed potatoes.

(145)

## STUFFED BURGER ROLL EPICURE
*Serves 6*

Mix 1½ pounds of lean raw ground beef; 1 scant tablespoon of grated onion; 1 scant tablespoon of chopped parsley; 3 slices of bacon, ground; and 1 scant teaspoon each of sage, sugar, and prepared mustard. Set aside while preparing the following stuffing.

*Sage Dressing.* Mix 1 cup of cracker crumbs, ½ cup of butter melted in ⅓ cup of boiling water, and salt and pepper to taste. Season with ½ teaspoon of powdered sage and 1 pinch of summer savory or marjoram.

Place a sheet of wax paper on the table. Spread the burger mixture to roughly about 6 inches by 8 inches. Then place another sheet of wax paper on top of the mixture. With a rolling pin, roll the mixture to medium thin, approximately 12 by 8 inches. Pull off the top paper carefully. Make a rough cylinder of the sage dressing, about 6 inches long. Place it at one end of the burger, and carefully roll, pulling away the bottom sheet of wax paper. Wrap the roll in buttered wax paper. Place in a Dutch oven. Add 1 cup of meat stock, canned bouillon, or water and a bouquet garni composed of 6 sprigs of fresh parsley, 1 large bay leaf, 3 sprigs of green celery tops, and 1 sprig of thyme, tied together with white thread. Adjust the lid, and set the Dutch oven in a moderate oven (375 degrees F.) for 1½ hours. Serve with cranberry sauce, baked potatoes, and a green salad, and you have a meal fit for a king.

*In the early eighteenth century, French Acadians in the lowlands of Nova Scotia were as skilled in making dikes as the Dutch. The dikes were necessary to protect the many fertile fields growing "bread corn" from flooding.*

### SWISS BURGER SQUARE                              (146)
Serves 6

Mix lightly 1½ pounds of twice-ground lean raw beef chuck; ½ pound of meat sausage; 1¾ teaspoons of salt; ½ teaspoon of black pepper, coarsely and freshly ground; 2 tablespoons of grated onion; 2 tablespoons of chopped parsley; 2 whole fresh eggs, slightly beaten into ⅓ cup of tomato juice; and 1 cup of corn flakes. Add more tomato juice if the mixture is a little stiff. Spread 1½ inches thick in a generously greased shallow pan. Bake in a moderately hot oven (375 degrees F.) for 30 minutes, or until the edges are beginning to crisp. Serve with your favorite brown gravy.

PART TWO

# Burger Loaves

Burger Loaves—with Cheese—Fruit—Macaroni—Sour Cream—
Vegetables—Wine—Including Layer—Pinwheel—Ribbon—Ring
Forms

On Sunday a cut from a Sirloin,
On Monday cold ditto will do,
On Tuesday a Hash, or Sausage and Mash,
On Wednesday a good Beef Stew.

Don't fill up your belly with buns, milk and jelly,
Have something with sustenance—do!
For troubles will fly, on a steak and kid pie,
So have meat every day on your menu.

OLD LONDON SONG

# BURGER LOAVES

**M**eat loaf may be a homely dish, but when well made, it is a deservedly popular one, and one that lovers of good food relish more than elaborate concoctions. Almost any meat may be used, of course, but the best meat loaves are made from uncooked meat that is very finely ground or chopped. It can be such an interesting dish if you will but exert your originality.

Actually, there are as many burger loaf recipes as there are cooks who make them. It is the bit of seasoning, the combination of meats, the way they're baked, that makes these recipes varied and interesting. Another trick for introducing variety is in the baking. If you like lots of crust, shape the mixture in a roll or loaf, and bake it in a flat pan with a few strips of bacon over the top. If your like less crust, bake it in a deep bread pan lined with wax paper or parchment, which facilitates removing the loaf whole.

One of the most important points in making burger loaf juicy and tender is to bake it slowly, for at least an hour or more, basting it with some soup or its own drippings. This slow baking is always the secret of success.

Ever have a meat loaf crumble like hash when it is sliced? Just fool it by adding a little cooked tapioca when it is put together. That will hold it.

You may be ritzy with a meat loaf. Bake the loaf first, place on a plank, surround it with small cooked onions, tomato halves sprinkled with buttered crumbs, and mounds of fluffy mashed potatoes. Season and place in the oven until the potatoes and crumbed tomatoes are lightly browned. Garnish with parsley and serve with a crisp salad.

And remember that burger meat is also delicious as a stuffing for vegetables, such as green peppers, large baked onions, large turnips, or large tomatoes, or in combination with other foods. Ever try serving eggplant stuffed with burger meat, or a burger mold in a rice ring?

A burger loaf that is good served hot from the oven loses none of its tempting flavor after it has cooled. Most homemakers take advantage of this during warm weather, and plan an extra amount of the family's favorite burger loaf to take care of two meals.

Few foods are more versatile than burger loaves. They can be baked in large ring molds, in muffin pans to make individual loaves, or in bread pans. A stuffing in a burger loaf plays a double role. It adds a decorative appearance when the meat is sliced, and helps to make the meat mixture serve more persons. Hard-cooked eggs placed lengthwise through the center of the meat before baking are most attractive.

Beef and pork make one of the best combinations because the fat of the pork supplements that of the beef. For a more delicately flavored loaf, use veal to replace part of the beef. Another favorite mixture is made from smoked ham. Most people prefer to use it combined half and half with fresh beef, or veal, or veal and fresh pork combined.

One pound of ground meat serves four persons, even without the addition of crumbs or vegetables. But remember that all ground burger, be it beef, pork, veal, or ham, is tender before it is cooked, but you can toughen it easily by overcooking.

A burger loaf will slice even at the piping-hot stage, if it is bound with a combination of thick sauce alone, or with some starchy substance, such as bread crumbs, cooked rice, or mashed potatoes. Such ingredients serve a double purpose, making the loaf or the burger cake less compact, yet binding the tiniest pieces of meat together.

Variation of the foundation for meat loaf yields many an interesting, hearty main dish, hot or cold, according to taste or season. Variation begins, of course, with some change in the meat, which in the standard recipe for burger loaf is beef, and seasonings. Part of the meat may be replaced by ham, lamb, liver, pork, or sausage. The extending ingredients, eggs, milk, cracker or bread crumbs, and cereal, may be varied. Stuffing also may be used as an extender, as well as for variation. Simmering or steaming the burger mixture in a loaf, a ring mold, individual loaves, or cones, gives a different product from that baked in a loaf pan.

(147)

BURGER BANANA LOAF
*West Indies method—serves 6 generously*

Mix 2 pounds of lean raw ground beef; 1 cup of celery, diced small, using the stalk and leaves; 1 cup of bread or cracker crumbs; salt, pepper, and a dash of powdered nutmeg to taste; and 1 whole fresh egg and 1 fresh egg yolk, slightly beaten. Blend thoroughly. Divide the mixture into two equal parts. Pack one part in a generously greased loaf pan. Cream or dice small 3 ripe bananas. Mix with 1 generous tablespoon of lemon juice and ½ cup of cracker or bread crumbs. Season to taste with salt and pepper and a dash of chili or cayenne pepper. Spread the banana mixture on top of the mixture in the loaf pan as evenly as possible. Over this, lay 4 or 5 slices of bacon, pan broiled and well drained. (You may omit bacon, if desired.) Over the bacon or the banana mixture, pack the second part of the meat mixture. Over the meat, lay 4 or 5 slices of raw bacon. Bake in a moderate oven (350–375 degrees F.) for 45 to 50 minutes, placing a buttered paper on top, if the bacon browns too fast. Unmold on a hot platter, and serve at once with a green salad.

*Polite Egyptian hosts of 1100 b.c. did not dine with their guests, but ate afterward. During banquets, they supervised the service, making sure that everyone was well fed.*

(148)

BURGER BAY-LEAF LOAF
*Western method—serves 6 generously*

Mix and blend thoroughly 2 pounds of lean raw ground beef; 1 cup of cracker crumbs; 1¼ cups of tomato juice; 1 teaspoon of poultry seasoning; 1 large onion, grated; 2 tablespoons of parsley, minced fine; 1 medium-sized green pepper, free from seeds and white ribs, and chopped fine; 1 clove of garlic, chopped very fine; salt, pepper, and nutmeg to taste; 1 tablespoon of Worcestershire sauce; and 1 whole fresh egg, slightly beaten. Divide the mixture into two parts. Pack one part in a generously greased loaf pan. (Bacon drippings give a fine flavor.) Over this, lay 2 hard-cooked eggs, chopped fine. Then spread the remaining part over the eggs. Top with 5 medium-sized bay leaves. Bake for 1 hour in a very moderate oven (325 degrees F.). Serve unmolded, after removing the bay leaves, on a hot platter with your favorite tomato sauce.

### BURGER CORN LOAF (149)
*Serves 6 generously*

Mix together 1¼ pounds of lean raw ground beef and ½ pound of lean raw ground pork. Put again through a food chopper. Then add 1 large onion, grated; 2 tablespoons of chopped chives or parsley; 1½ or more teaspoons of salt; ¼ teaspoon of freshly ground pepper; 1 whole fresh egg and 1 fresh egg yolk, slightly beaten together; ½ cup of soft bread crumbs, ½ teaspoon of poultry seasoning; 1 teaspoon each of Worcestershire and A-1 sauce; and 1 large can of corn (2½ cups). Divide the mixture into two equal parts. Pack one part in a generously greased loaf pan. Lay over it 4 slices of raw bacon, or still better, 4 thin slices of parboiled salt pork (in such case, reduce the amount of salt). Over this, pack the remaining burger. Lastly, place on top 4 slices of bacon or salt pork. Bake about 1 hour in a moderate oven (350 degrees F.). Pour off the excess fat. Invert on a hot platter. Let stand for a few minutes to set. Lift off the pan, and serve as hot as possible.

### BURGER CURRIED LOAF (150)
*Serves 6 generously*

Mix 1½ pounds of lean raw ground beef; 3 lamb kidneys, parboiled, then ground, removing all nerves and skins; 1 cup of soft bread crumbs; 2 tablespoons of grated onion; 2 tablespoons of parsley, finely chopped; 1 whole fresh egg, slightly beaten; 2 teaspoons of Worcestershire sauce; 2 teaspoons of curry powder, mixed with the Worcestershire sauce; 1 generous teaspoon of salt, or more; ¼ generous teaspoon of pepper; ½ teaspoon of mace; a grating of nutmeg; and ½ teaspoon of poultry seasoning. Blend thoroughly, and pack into a loaf pan, generously greased with bacon drippings or ham fat. Lay over the top 4 slices of bacon. Bake about 1¼ hours in a very moderate oven (325 degrees F.). Pour off the excess fat. Invert the loaf pan. Let stand for a few minutes to set. Lift off the pan, and serve very hot with your favorite tomato or mushroom sauce.

Spanish explorers in Mexico in 1522 found the natives using a hard cheeselike pudding as money as well as for rations. A day's labor was rated at eight puddings.

(151)

## BURGER, CARROT, AND BANANA LOAF
*Serves 6 generously*

Mix thoroughly 1½ pounds of lean raw ground beef; 2 medium-sized bananas, mashed; 1¼ cups of grated raw carrot; 1 large onion, grated; 1½ tablespoons of parsley, finely chopped; 1 whole fresh egg, slightly beaten; 2 teaspoons of salt; ¼ generous teaspoon of pepper; ½ teaspoon of mace; and a grating of nutmeg. Pack the mixture into a generously greased loaf pan. Spread over ¼ cup of tomato catsup. Bake for 1¼ long hours in a moderate oven (350 degrees F.). Invert the pan on a hot platter. Let stand for a few minutes to set. Lift the pan. Serve at once surrounded with a mixture of mashed potatoes and rutabagas in equal parts.

(152)

## BURGER AND HAM LOAF
*Serves 6 generously*

Mix 1½ pounds of lean raw ground beef; ⅓ pound of lean raw ground ham; ½ cup of cracker crumbs; 2 teaspoons of salt, or more; ¼ teaspoon of pepper; 1 teaspoon of Worcestershire sauce; 2 table-spoons of grated onion; 1 tablespoon of parsley, minced fine; 1 whole fresh egg, slightly beaten; a grating of nutmeg; and ½ teaspoon of poultry seasoning. Shape into a loaf, handling lightly. Place the loaf in a large baking pan. Pour around it ½ to ¾ cup of meat stock, bouillon, or water, mixed with 2 teaspoons of prepared mustard. Add a bouquet garni composed of 1 bay leaf, 6 sprigs of parsley, and 1 sprig of thyme, tied together with thread; 1 slice of onion; 2 whole cloves; and 2 sprigs of green celery tops. Bake for 45 to 50 minutes, basting frequently with the liquid in the pan, in a moderately hot oven (350 degrees F.). The liquid in the pan is the base for a fine piquant sauce, which may be thickened with a little flour after the loaf has been transferred to a hot platter. Pour the sauce over the loaf, and serve at once. You may garnish the platter with fruits.

While a chef today is readily identified by his tall white cap, Italian chefs of the twelfth century began a tradition of carrying tiny pots on long handles in public, much as soldiers carry swagger sticks.

## BURGER HORSERADISH LOAF (153)
*Serves 6 generously*

In a mixing bowl, put 2 pounds of lean raw ground beef; ¼ pound of salt pork, parboiled or scalded, then ground; ¼ cup of grated onion; ¼ teaspoon of marjoram; ¼ teaspoon of thyme leaves; 1 teaspoon of prepared mustard; ½ cup of soft bread or cracker crumbs; 2 scant teaspoons of salt; 2 whole fresh eggs, slightly beaten; ¼ teaspoon of freshly ground black pepper; ½ cup of prepared horseradish; ½ cup of tomato catsup; and 2 tablespoons of parsley, finely chopped. Blend thoroughly, and shape into a loaf. Place in a greased baking pan. Surround with ¼ cup of tomato juice, well mixed with ½ cup of meat stock, canned bouillon, or water. Add 1 bay leaf, 4 sprigs of green celery tops, and 1 branch of thyme, tied together with thread; 1 slice of onion; and 1 very small clove of garlic, crushed. Place over it 4 or 5 strips of raw bacon. Bake for 1 long hour, or until the bacon is done, in a moderate oven, basting frequently with the liquid in the pan. Carefully transfer to a hot platter. Drain part of the fat from the gravy, and add ½ cup of bouillon in which has been diluted 2 teaspoons of flour. Bring to a boil while scraping the pan with a wooden spoon. Strain over the meat loaf, and serve at once, with a side dish of generously buttered noodles and a green and fruit salad.

## BURGER-CHEESE LAYER LOAF (154)
*Farmer method—serves 6 generously*

Put in a mixing bowl 2 cups of grated raw carrots, 1 cup of strained then sieved cottage cheese, and 1 cup of soft bread crumbs. Bind with 1 whole fresh egg and 1 egg yolk, slightly beaten. Season with salt, pepper, and 1 teaspoon of Worcestershire sauce. Press the mixture into a buttered loaf pan. Mix well 2 pounds of twice-ground lean raw beef; 1 teaspoon of A-1 sauce; a few drops of Tabasco sauce; 3 tablespoons of catsup; 1 whole fresh egg, slightly beaten; ¼ cup of soft bread crumbs; salt, pepper, and nutmeg to taste; and lastly ½ cup of cracklings (rendered pork cubes). Blend thoroughly, and pack over the cheese mixture, pressing firmly. Unmold on a greased baking pan. Bake for 1 hour in a moderate oven (350 degrees F.). Carefully transfer to a hot platter. Garnish with crisp watercress. Surround the loaf with ½ cup of chili sauce, heated to the boiling point with an equal part of rich bouillon, meat stock, or rich consommé, highly seasoned.

(155)

## BURGER LIVER LOAF
*Serves 6 generously*

Remove the skin and tubes from ½ pound of sliced beef liver. Sear on both sides in 1 generous tablespoon of bacon drippings. Lift out the liver, place it on a hot platter, and keep it warm. Then grind it and mix it with 1 whole fresh egg, slightly beaten and mixed with any liver juice, and salt and pepper to taste. Add 1 cup of soft bread or cracker crumbs; ½ cup of cold sweet milk; ¼ teaspoon of sage; ¼ teaspoon of thyme leaves; 2 tablespoons of grated onion; 1 blade of garlic, mashed; 2 tablespoons of parsley, minced fine; and more milk, to make a rather moist mixture. Set aside. Mix 1½ pounds of lean raw ground beef with salt and pepper, and 1 teaspoon of Worcestershire sauce, beaten with 1 whole fresh egg.

Place half the burger mixture in the bottom of a generously greased loaf pan. Spread the liver mixture over as evenly as possible. Cover with the remaining burger mixture. Then top with 4 or 5 slices of raw bacon. Bake for 50 minutes to 1 hour in a moderate oven (350 degrees F.). Serve unmolded on a hot platter, surrounded with watercress. Tomato, mushroom, or brown sauce may be served on the side.

*Virginia planters of colonial days did not pay their pastor with money but with food. The usual contribution was "three hammes and a parssel of pottattues the month."*

(156)

## BURGER-ONION LAYER LOAF
*Serves 6 generously*

Season 2 pounds of lean raw ground beef with salt and pepper to taste. Mix with 2 cups of grated raw carrots; 2 tablespoons of parsley, minced; 1 tablespoon of Worcestershire sauce; ¼ teaspoon each of thyme leaves, marjoram, and sage. Divide into two equal parts, and pack one part in the bottom of a greased loaf pan. Spread over 1 cup of thinly sliced smothered onion made as indicated for recipe No. 29. Top with the remaining meat mixture. Pour over 3 generous tablespoons of tomato catsup. Bake for 1 hour in a moderate oven. Serve the loaf on a hot platter, surrounded with brown sauce.

## BURGER LOAF WITH VEGETABLES     (157)
*Serves 6 generously*

If you relish meat in meat dishes, with appropriate vegetable concomitants—and have courage to fly in the face of convention—try a meat and vegetable loaf, and forget the bread crumbs. A dish of quails on toast cannot be compared with this meat loaf, as made in France.

Mix together 2 pounds of coarsely ground lean raw round of beef; 2 tablespoons of ground beef suet; 2 medium-sized onions, grated; 1 large can of tomatoes, pulp broken; 1 pound of fresh string beans, coarsely ground or chopped; 6 stalks of celery, coarsely ground or chopped; ½ pound of fresh mushrooms, coarsely chopped; 2 tablespoons of butter; 2 medium-sized raw carrots, coarsely grated; and 3 tablespoons of parsley, minced. Toss them again and again until they are thoroughly mixed. Then add 2 whole fresh eggs, slightly beaten; 1 tablespoon of salt; 6 or 8 freshly ground whole peppercorns; ½ teaspoon of thyme leaves; ¼ teaspoon of dry mustard; and ½ cup of soy sauce or 2 tablespoons of Worcestershire sauce.

Now separate the yolks and whites of 2 fresh eggs, beat the yolks slightly with ½ cup of fresh milk or undiluted evaporated milk, and add to the mixture. Blend well, using a wooden spoon and fork.

Line a large baking dish or deep soufflé dish, bottom and sides, with very thin slices of bacon, close together, but not overlapping one another. Beat the 2 egg whites stiff, but not dry, and fold them gently into the meat and vegetable mixture. Turn this into the bacon-lined dish. If it has a cover, so much the better. The ideal setup for the cooking of the loaf is a Dutch oven in which the baking dish, with a cover, fits handily. Otherwise, cover the baking dish, and place it in a pan of hot water in a hot oven (400 degrees F.). Do not let the water boil away; replenish when necessary with boiling water. When this is all cooking briskly, reduce the heat to 325–350 degrees F., and let simmer for 2 long hours.

Meanwhile, prepare a roux with 1½ tablespoons of flour and 2 tablespoons of butter, and brown lightly. (A roux is a mixture of flour and butter or other fat, blended together over a gentle flame until slightly browned, or well browned, according to directions.) Uncover the baking dish, and you will discover that the loaf has shrunk away from the sides and is almost floating in a sea of rich and delicious sauce. Carefully drain off the sauce, and thicken it with the roux. Then, and this is the most important of all, turn out the loaf on a fireproof serving dish, peel off the strips of bacon, and arrange them around the loaf. Put the dish in a very hot oven (550 degrees F.), or under the flame of the broiling oven, and brown the surface quickly without drying it. The bacon will be dried off and crisp at the same time. Serve in the hot dish, after garnishing the loaf with a glazing of the sauce and with sprigs of watercress. Serve the rich sauce, which will be abundant, in a gravy boat.

*In 1886, a group of Boston restaurants tried to sell lifetime "meal tickets" good for three meals a day and a choice of the menu for life. They were priced at $15 each. None was sold.*

(158)

## BURGER LOAF BOHEMIAN METHOD
*Hovezí sekaninas—serves 6 generously*

As a province of the old empire of Austria-Hungary, Bohemia was for many years noted as the home of culinary delicacies. Bohemian cookery is necessarily a mixture of German, Hungarian, and Austrian methods of preparing food. There is a touch of the Slav, as in so many other countries of southeastern Europe, and perhaps it is this slight suggestion of oriental flavor that has made Bohemian dishes so popular.

In the rural sections, where most of the famous Bohemian dishes originated, there is little formality in cooking. Cookbooks are uncommon. The recipes, so popular today, have been handed down verbally through generations. The savoriness of Bohemian cooking is still appreciated all over the world, even though the dishes do not represent any distinct nationality.

Mix together 2 pounds of lean raw ground beef; 4 slices of bacon, finely chopped; 2 or 3 tablespoons of bread crumbs, soaked in 2 or 3 tablespoons of sweet cold milk; 2 whole fresh eggs, slightly beaten; salt and pepper to taste; and ¼ teaspoon of sage, blending well. Pack the mixture into a generously buttered loaf pan. Sprinkle 2 tablespoons of fine bread crumbs on top. Bake in a moderate oven (350 degrees F.) for 1½ hours, basting occasionally with ¼ cup of melted butter. Serve hot or cold as, in fact, any kind of meat loaf.

## BURGER LOAF COTTAGE METHOD (159)
*Serves 6 generously*

Line a loaf pan with bacon strips on the bottom only. Over the bacon, pack the following mixture. Mix thoroughly 1½ pounds of twice-ground lean raw beef; 1 cup of cooked rice; 2 tablespoons of grated onion; 2 tablespoons of minced parsley or 1 tablespoon each of parsley and chopped green celery tops; 1½ or more teaspoons of salt; ¼ teaspoon of black pepper; ¼ teaspoon each of sage and marjoram; 1 whole fresh egg, beaten with 1 fresh egg yolk; and ½ cup (more or less) of cold rich milk. Pack the burger mixture into a generously greased loaf pan, and press in it, burying completely, 3 hard-cooked eggs, halved. Pour over 4 tablespoons of tomato catsup. Bake for 1 hour in a moderate oven (350 degrees F.). Serve hot or cold, serve with creamed spinach and French fried potatoes.

## BURGER LOAF COUNTRY METHOD I (160)
*Serves 6 generously*

Heat 2 tablespoons of ground beef suet in a large skillet, and slightly brown in it 2 medium-sized onions and 1 large green pepper, free from seeds and white ribs, both minced fine. Turn this into a mixing bowl. Add ½ pound of pot cheese; 1½ pounds of twice-ground lean raw beef; ¼ teaspoon of chili powder; 6 black olives, pitted, then ground; ¼ cup of nut meats, ground; 1 large can of tomatoes; 1 package of noodles, cooked and well drained;

2 whole fresh eggs, slightly beaten; 1¾ or more teaspoons of salt; and ½ teaspoon of black pepper. Blend thoroughly, and to insure smoothness and lightness, put once more through a food chopper. Pack the mixture into a generously buttered loaf pan. Cover with a buttered paper. Bake for 1½ hours in a moderate oven (350 degrees F.), removing the buttered paper 20 minutes before the loaf is done. Unmold on a hot platter, and serve with a side dish of tomato sauce and a green salad.

(161)

## BURGER LOAF COUNTRY METHOD II
*Serves 6 generously*

Mix well 1 pound of lean raw ground beef, ¾ pound of lean raw ground veal, and 2 or 3 ounces of ground salt pork with 2 whole fresh eggs, slightly beaten with ¾ teaspoon of salt, ½ teaspoon of thyme, ½ cup of cold sweet milk, 2 tablespoons of finely chopped celery, lastly, beating in 1 generous teaspoon of lemon juice. Pack in a generously greased loaf pan, and bake for 1½ hours in a moderately slow oven (325 degrees F.). Unmold onto a hot platter, and pour over the following sauce.

*Horseradish Sauce.* Add 1 can of condensed mushroom soup to ½ cup of brown gravy. Bring to a boil, stirring occasionally. Slowly stir in 1 tablespoon of brown sugar diluted in 2 tablespoons of meat stock or hot water, 1 generous teaspoon of dry mustard, and 3 tablespoons of prepared horseradish. Beat well. Then stir in 2 egg yolks, one at a time, beating well over a low flame, but do not allow to boil.

In 545 A.D., *King Totila of Italy paid Isaac Le Capenus, a Byzantine, 7000 gold pieces for an oriental cookbook containing 2000 recipes.*

(162)

## BURGER LOAF CLUB METHOD I
*Serves 6 generously*

Prepare a stuffing as follows. Toss together 3½ cups of soft bread crumbs; salt and pepper to taste; 1 large onion, grated; 2 tablespoons of parsley, chopped; 1 teaspoon of sage; and 1 tablespoon of ground beef suet. Moisten with ¾ cup of cold sweet milk, and season with additional salt and pepper to taste. Divide the stuffing in two parts. Place half of it in a buttered casserole, forming a round flat patty. Over this, flatten ¾ pound of lean raw ground beef, seasoned to taste with salt and pepper, and mixed with 1 teaspoon of Worcestershire sauce and 1 pinch of thyme. Over this, arrange another patty of the stuffing. Then over the stuffing, a patty made of ½ pound of lean raw ground beef mixed with ¼ pound of meat sausage. Spread over this ¼ cup of tomato catsup. Place a buttered paper over all, and bake about 1¾ hours in a slow oven (300 degrees F.), removing the paper 20 minutes before the loaf is done. Invert on a hot platter, cut into wedges, and serve with caper sauce.

*Caper Sauce.* Melt 2 tablespoons of butter, and stir in 2 tablespoons of flour. Season with ½ teaspoon of salt, 1 tablespoon of minced onion, and ⅛ teaspoon of pepper. Stir the mixture until thoroughly blended. Slowly pour in 1 cup of hot meat stock, canned bouillon, or 2 bouillon cubes dissolved in 1 cup of boiling water, stirring constantly over a gentle flame until the sauce is smooth and thick. Then add 1 tablespoon of vinegar and 2 tablespoons of capers. Cook for 2 minutes, stirring occasionally.

## BURGER LOAF CLUB METHOD II (163)
*Serves 6 generously*

Heat 3 tablespoons of fat. Add 1 quart of thinly sliced onions, and toss gently until they are coated with the fat. Cover, and place over a low flame to steam for 8 to 10 minutes, shaking the pan frequently. Lightly mix 2 pounds of lean raw ground beef; 2 scant teaspoons of salt; ¼ teaspoon of black pepper; 1 small green pepper, chopped; 6 black olives, chopped; and ¼ teaspoon each of sage and thyme. Divide into two parts. Place one part in the bottom of a generously greased loaf pan, and spread 1 tablespoon of prepared mustard over the top. Cover with half of the onions. Place the second part on top of the onions. Spread with 1 tablespoon of prepared mustard, then with the remaining onions. Pour the fat in which the onions were steamed around the burger, and stick 6 whole cloves on the top alternately with 4 bay leaves. Bake in a very hot oven (425 degrees F.) about 10 minutes. Reduce the temperature to moderate (375 degrees F.), and continue baking for

50 minutes, or until the meat is done. Serve on a hot platter with a garnish of baked tomatoes and parsley. Brown gravy may be prepared from the fat in the pan, if desired.

(164)

## BURGER LOAF FARMER METHOD
*Serves 6 generously*

Mix together 2 pounds of lean raw ground beef; ½ pound of salt pork, ground; 2 whole fresh eggs, slightly beaten in 1 cup of milk; 3 tablespoons of butter, melted; and 3 tablespoons of tomato catsup. Season with 1 scant tablespoon of salt, 2 tablespoons of finely minced onion, and 1 tablespoon of finely minced parsley, and blend together with 1 scant cup of bread crumbs. Shape into a loaf. Cover with 6 strips of bacon. Bake in a moderate oven (375 degrees F.) for 1¼ to 1½ hours, basting frequently with the fat and liquid coming from the loaf. Serve with a side dish of brown piquant sauce.

*Brown Piquant Sauce.* Melt 2 tablespoons of butter or drippings, and stir in 2 tablespoons of flour. Season with salt and pepper to taste. When well blended and brown, stir in 1 cup of meat stock gradually. Stir over a low flame until smooth and thick. Let boil for 1 minute. Then stir in 1 tablespoon of vinegar, 1 tablespoon of chopped onion, 1 tablespoon of capers, 1 tablespoon of minced pickles, and 1 tablespoon of minced olives. Bring to a boil, and serve.

*In the twelfth century, an English innkeeper for a sum equivalent to a quarter would feed a family of five for a week.*

(165)

## BURGER LOAF FLORIDA METHOD
*Serves 6 generously*

In a mixing bowl, place 2 pounds of lean raw ground beef; ½ pound of lean ground pork; 2 whole fresh eggs, slightly beaten; 1 scant cup of grapefruit juice; 1 cup of bread crumbs; 1 tablespoon each of grated onion and minced parsley; salt and pepper to taste; and ¼ teaspoon each of sage, mace, and marjoram. Blend thoroughly, but lightly. Place in a generously greased loaf pan or mold. Set in a shallow pan of hot water, and bake for 1¼ hours in a moderate oven (350 degrees F.). Serve with a side dish of raisin gravy.

*Raisin Gravy.* Heat 3 tablespoons of fat (any kind desired) and 2 tablespoons of browned flour. Stir in 2 cups of hot water or canned bouillon; 2 tablespoons of seedless raisins, parboiled and drained; 1 pinch of cinnamon; and 1 teaspoon of drained prepared horseradish. Bring to a boil, and let simmer for a few minutes, stirring occasionally.

*Browned Flour.* Place any amount desired of flour on a shallow pan or a pie plate, spreading as evenly as possible. Set in a low oven (300 degrees F.), stirring frequently until the flour turns a delicate brown. Keep this in a closed jar, in a cool dry place. This will keep for months, and is handy for thickening sauces, stews, and even soups.

(166)

## BURGER LOAF HOME METHOD I
*Serves 6 generously*

Try out 2 thin slices of salt pork, diced small, until golden brown. Add the pork cracklings and drippings to 2 pounds of lean raw ground beef; ½ cup of quick-cooking tapioca; 2 tablespoons of grated onion; 1 tablespoon of chives, finely chopped; 2 cups of canned tomatoes; 2½ teaspoons of salt; and ¼ teaspoon each of pepper and nutmeg. Mix lightly, but thoroughly. Bake in a loaf pan, lined with greased paper, for 1¼ hours, or until done, in a moderate oven (350 degrees F.). Garnish with crisp watercress, and serve a side dish of your favorite tomato or mushroom sauce.

*No thirteenth-century Irish sea captain could get sailors for his ship until he provided enough food to feed the families of the men who were to sail with him.*

(167)

## BURGER LOAF HOME METHOD II
*Serves 6 generously*

Mix well ¾ pound of lean raw ground beef; ½ pound of lean fresh pork, ground; ¾ pound of smoked lean ham butt, ground; 1 generous cup of soft bread crumbs; 2 teaspoons of salt; ¼ teaspoon each of black pepper, powdered mustard, sage, and poultry seasoning; 1½ tablespoons of grated onion; 1½ tablespoons of minced parsley; and 2 whole fresh eggs, slightly beaten in 1 cup of cold sweet milk. Pack the mixture in a loaf pan, and bake for 1¼ hours in a moderate oven (350 degrees F.). Serve with this tomato catsup sauce.

*Tomato Catsup Sauce.* Melt 2 tablespoons of butter or margarine, and stir in 2 tablespoons of flour. Cook until the mixture begins to bubble and brown, stirring almost constantly. Then add ⅓ cup of tomato catsup, ½ cup of meat stock or water, 1 tablespoon of vinegar, 1 scant teaspoon of granulated sugar, and salt and black pepper to taste. Blend well, bring to the boiling point, then stir in 1 generous teaspoon of onion juice. Let simmer for 5 minutes, stirring frequently, until thick and well blended.

(168)

## BURGER LOAF NEW ENGLAND METHOD
*Serves 6 generously*

Arrange 8 strips of bacon in a greased loaf pan. Mix and blend well 1½ pounds of lean round beef, ground; 1 pound of lean raw pork, ground; 1 scant teaspoon of sage; ½ cup of celery, chopped, using stalks and leaves; 6 soda crackers, broken into small pieces; 3 tablespoons of butter or bacon drippings; 1 small green pepper, chopped; ½ cup of fresh or canned mushrooms, chopped; 1 medium-sized onion, chopped; 1 small clove of garlic, finely chopped; 2 generous teaspoons of salt; ¼ teaspoon each of thyme and cloves; and ½ cup of undiluted evaporated milk, mixed with 1 whole fresh egg, slightly beaten. Pack the mixture in the bacon-lined pan, and cover with 8 strips of bacon. Bake for 1½ hours in a moderate oven (350 degrees F.), covered with a buttered paper for 1 hour. Serve with a side dish of horseradish brown sauce.

*Horseradish Brown Sauce.* To 1½ cups of brown sauce, hot and simmering, and ½ generous cup of bread crumbs and 2 generous tablespoons of drained prepared horseradish. Boil once. Serve immediately,

(169)

## BURGER LOAF STEAMED METHOD
*Country style—serves 6 generously*

Cover 1 slice of bread with milk, then squeeze it dry. To the bread, add 1½ pounds of lean raw ground beef; ¼ pound of fresh pork, ground; ¼ pound of lean veal, ground; 2 tablespoons of grated onion; 2 tablespoons of ground dry green celery leaves; 1 tablespoon of parsley, chopped fine; 2 whole fresh eggs, slightly beaten in ¼ cup of thin sour cream; 1¾ teaspoons of salt; ¼ teaspoon of black pepper; ½ teaspoon of sage; and 2 tablespoons of chopped capers. Blend well, and shape into a round ball. Tie loosely in several thicknesses of scalded cheesecloth or in a damp floured towel, securing the ends with string. Simmer steadily for 1¾ hours, seeing that there is always enough rolling water to cover the loaf. Remove the cheesecloth or towel. Spice. Dress on a hot platter. Garnish with parsley or watercress, and pour over Lyonnaise sauce.

*Lyonnaise Sauce.* Cook very slowly, until blond, 2 medium-sized onions, finely chopped. Moisten with ½ cup of dry white wine, mixed with ½ cup of good wine vinegar. Let this reduce one-third over a bright flame. Then add, stirring briskly from the bottom of the saucepan, 1½ cups of rich brown sauce. (The original recipe calls for demiglace sauce, which is really too expensive.) Allow to simmer for 15 minutes. Then strain through a cloth or fine sieve. Season to taste with salt and pepper and a few drops of Tabasco sauce.

*Ancient Libyans eagerly hunted for hawks, the necks of which, when stuffed, were considered great delicacies. Oddly enough, according to Libyan law, only married men were permitted to eat them.*

(170)

## BURGER MACARONI LOAF DINNER
*Italian method—serves 6 generously*

Cook ½ package of macaroni in boiling salted water until tender, or about 10 to 12 minutes. Drain and rinse under cold water. Mix 1½ pounds of lean raw ground beef; 1 medium-sized onion, finely chopped; and 1 small green pepper, free from seeds and white ribs, then chopped fine; and 1 large clove of garlic, chopped very fine. Brown in 3 tablespoons of butter, stirring with a fork as it cooks. Season with salt, pepper, and 2 teaspoons of chopped fresh fennel. Blend well. Put a layer of seasoned macaroni in a generously oiled casserole. Over the macaroni, sprinkle a No. 2 can of green peas, seasoned with salt and pepper to taste. Over the peas, sprinkle 1 teaspoon of chopped dill, then cover with the burger mixture. Pour over 1 can of tomato soup. Dot with about 1 tablespoon of butter. Cover tightly, and set in a moderate oven (375 degrees F.) for 2 hours without disturbing. Serve right from the casserole.

(171)

## BURGER MUSHROOM-STUFFED LOAF
*Serves 6 generously*

Sauté ½ pound of fresh or canned mushrooms, ½ cup of finely sliced onions, ¼ cup of finely chopped green celery leaves, and 1 small green pepper, free from seeds and white ribs, in ¼ cup of butter or other fat for 7 or 8 minutes, stirring frequently. Then stir in ¾ cup of cooked rice or 1 cup of soft bread crumbs. Season with salt, pepper, and mace to taste. Cook for 2 or 3 minutes, stirring almost constantly. Set aside to cool a little.

Meanwhile, season to taste, with salt and pepper and a grating of nutmeg, 2 pounds of lean raw ground beef, and mix with 1 scant cup of tomato sauce. Pack in a greased loaf pan. Scoop out the center, and fill with mushroom stuffing. Close up, having the stuffing completely covered. Place 6 strips of bacon over the top, and bake for 1½ hours in a moderate oven (350 degrees F.). Serve hot with tomato sauce. Very fine when sliced cold and served with a green salad with mayonnaise.

(172)

## BURGER OYSTER LOAF I
*Maine method—serves 6 generously*

Mix thoroughly 2 pounds of lean raw ground beef, 1 cup of small oysters, whole and well drained, and ¼ cup of melted butter or margarine. Then mix with ¼ cup of grated or finely chopped onion; 2 tablespoons of finely minced parsley; 1½ tablespoons of finely minced celery leaves; ⅔ generous cup of tomato sauce or soup; 1¾ cups of soft bread crumbs; salt, pepper, nutmeg, and sage to taste; 1 teaspoon of paprika; and 1 teaspoon of prepared mustard. Mix well, and form in a loaf. Place on a baking sheet, and bake for 1¼ hours in a moderate oven (350 degrees F.), basting frequently with ¼ cup of tomato catsup, mixed with ¼ cup of tomato juice. Serve hot. The liquid in the pan may be used as a sauce, if desired.

BURGER OYSTER LOAF II                                    (173)
*Long Island method—serves 6 generously*

Mix well 1½ pounds of lean raw ground beef; ½ pound of lean raw ground veal; 1 cup of raw oysters, coarsely chopped; ¼ cup of drained canned mushrooms, chopped; 2 whole fresh eggs, slightly beaten in ⅓ cup of oyster liquor; ½ cup of soft bread crumbs; and salt, pepper, and mace to taste. Turn the mixture into a greased loaf pan, and bake for 1¼ hours in a moderate oven (350 degrees F.).

*Because of the servant problem in France between 1814 and 1825, polite society decreed that no dinner party should exceed four couples.*

BURGER PICKLE-STUFFED LOAF                              (174)
*New Jersey method—serves 6 generously*

Mix well ¾ cup of dry bread cubes, fried in bacon fat and thoroughly drained; 1 cup of scalded rich milk; 2 slightly beaten eggs; 2 teaspoons of salt, or more; ¼ teaspoon of black pepper; a few grains of cayenne pepper; ⅓ cup of chili sauce; ½ teaspoon of mace; ¼ teaspoon of thyme leaves; 1 pinch of chopped dill leaves; and 1¾ pounds of lean raw ground beef. Set aside while preparing the pickle stuffing.

*Pickle Stuffing.* Mix well ½ cup of onions, chopped fine; ¼ cup of butter or bacon drippings; 1¾ cups of soft bread crumbs; ⅔ cup of chopped sweet-sour pickles; salt and pepper to taste; ¼ teaspoon of sage; and ¼ teaspoon of clove.

Place half the burger mixture in a greased loaf pan. Cover with all the pickle stuffing, then with the remaining burger mixture. Pour over 3 to 4 tablespoons of tomato catsup. Over this, place 4 or 5 strips of raw bacon. Bake for 1¼ hours in a moderate oven (350 degrees F.), covered with a buttered paper, removing the paper 25 minutes before the loaf is done. Serve very hot with your favorite brown sauce.

BURGER PINWHEEL LOAF I                                  (175)
*Carrot stuffing—serves 6 generously*

Mix 2 pounds of lean raw ground beef, 2 teaspoons of salt or more, ½ teaspoon of black pepper, ½ teaspoon of thyme, ½ teaspoon of sage, ¼ teaspoon of marjoram, and 2 whole fresh eggs, slightly beaten with 3 tablespoons of tomato juice. After blending well, set aside while preparing the carrot stuffing.

*Carrot Stuffing.* Mix well 1 cup of soft bread crumbs and 1¾ cups of shredded raw carrots. Season to taste with salt, pepper, and 1 tablespoon of parsley. Blend in 1 tablespoon of bacon drippings (more or less).

Roll the burger mixture on a sheet of wax paper, with a wet rolling pin, about ¾ inch thick. Place the stuffing over the meat, then roll up like a jelly roll. Place in a baking pan, with ¼ cup of good beef stock, canned consommé, or water in bottom, and bake for 1¼ hours in a moderate oven (350 degrees F.). Serve with your favorite tomato or brown sauce.

(176)

## BURGER PINWHEEL LOAF II
*Savory corn-bread stuffing—serves 6 generously*

For the meat mixture, proceed as indicated in the above recipe (No. 175).

*Savory Corn-Bread Stuffing.* Mix well 1 cup of corn-bread crumbs; 4 tablespoons of bacon drippings; 1 medium-sized onion, grated; ½ cup of green celery tops, finely chopped; 1 tablespoon of minced parsley; ½ generous teaspoon of poultry seasoning; ¼ scant teaspoon of nutmeg; ¼ scant teaspoon of thyme; salt and pepper to taste; and ½ teaspoon of Worcestershire sauce, diluted in 1 whole fresh egg, slightly beaten with 1 tablespoon of milk.

Roll the burger mixture on a sheet of wax paper, with a wet rolling pin, about ¾ inch thick. Spread with the corn-bread stuffing, and roll up like a jelly roll. Place in a baking pan, the bottom of which is covered with ¼ generous cup of meat stock, canned bouillon, or water in which 1 bouillon cube has been dissolved. Bake for 1¼ hours in a moderate oven (350 degrees F.). Serve with a gravy made with the drippings in the pan.

(177)

## BURGER RIBBON LOAF
*Serves 6 generously*

Combine ¾ pound of lean raw ground beef; salt and pepper to taste; 1 whole fresh egg, slightly beaten; 3 tablespoons of soft bread crumbs; and 2 tablespoons of chili sauce. Set aside.

Combine ¾ pound of lean raw ground pork, 1 tablespoon of grated onion, 1 tablespoon of finely minced parsley, salt and pepper to taste, ½ teaspoon of sage, and 1 pinch of thyme. Moisten with 1 whole fresh egg, slightly beaten, mixed with 3 tablespoons of tomato catsup and 2 tablespoons of water. Set aside.

Combine ½ pound of lean raw ground veal; 3 strips of bacon, chopped very fine, preferably ground; salt and pepper to taste; 3 tablespoons soft bread crumbs; 1 teaspoon of Worcestershire sauce; and 1 whole fresh egg, well beaten with 3 tablespoons of milk.

Now spread the beef mixture in the bottom of a generously greased loaf pan. Over this, spread the pork mixture. Then over the pork, spread the veal mixture, pressing well and evenly. Top with 4 or 5 strips of raw bacon. Dot here and there with 4 whole cloves. Sprinkle with a large dry bay leaf, broken in bits. Place the loaf pan in a pan containing hot water, and bake, covered, for 1½ hours. Remove the cover, and continue baking for 25 to 30 minutes longer. Invert the pan over a hot platter. Let stand for a few minutes, then lift the pan. Serve surrounded with plenty of crisp watercress. No sauce is needed, because the loaf should be moist and juicy.

*Tuition fees were not paid in cash to New England schools and schoolmasters in the early part of the eighteenth century. For first year Latin, the cost was "ten stoute fowls, a half dozen jugs of sider and three hammes."*

BURGER RING LOAF                                                    (178)
*Home method—serves 6 generously*

Combine 2 cups of cooked rice; 2 pounds of lean raw ground beef; ¼ pound of meat sausage; ½ teaspoon of sage; ¼ teaspoon of thyme; 2 whole fresh eggs, well beaten with 1 cup of milk; salt and pepper to taste; 2 tablespoons of grated onion; and 2 tablespoons of chopped parsley. Blend thoroughly. Pack lightly in a generously greased ring mold. Cover with a buttered paper, and bake for 1 long hour in a moderate oven (350 degrees F.). Invert the mold on a hot large round platter, and fill the center with creamed spinach. Serve at once. Other kinds of cooked vegetables may be substituted, such as creamed peas, stewed tomatoes, or stewed potatoes.

(179)

## BURGER ROLLED-OATS LOAF
*Serves 6 generously*

Mix well, but lightly, 2 pounds of lean raw ground beef; 3 strips of raw bacon, ground; 2¾ teaspoons of salt; ⅓ teaspoon of black pepper; ¼ teaspoon of nutmeg; ¼ teaspoon of mace; ¼ cup of grated onion; 2 tablespoons of chopped parsley; 2 tablespoons of chopped green celery leaves; 1 cup of rolled oats; a No. 2 can of tomatoes; and 1 whole fresh egg, well beaten. Form into a loaf and pack in a greased loaf pan. Crisscross the surface with a knife, and bake for 1½ hours in a moderate oven (350 degrees F.). Serve with your favorite brown sauce.

(180)

## BURGER SALAMI LOAF
*Steamed method—serves 6 generously*

Remove the casing from ¼ pound of salami, slice it thin, and dice it very small. Then combine it with 1¼ pounds of lean raw ground beef chuck; ½ scant pound of lean raw ground veal; ¾ cup of soft bread crumbs; 2 tablespoons of grated onion; 2 tablespoons of chopped green celery leaves; 1 tablespoon of chopped parsley; 2 whole fresh eggs, slightly beaten with 1 cup of sweet cold milk; salt and black pepper to taste; and ¼ teaspoon each of sage, thyme, and cloves. Mix lightly but thoroughly with a fork. Gently press the burger mixture into a generously greased ring mold. Cover with waxed paper, tie securely, and place in a steamer. Cover tightly, and steam steadily for 2 hours, seeing that there is always boiling water covering the mold. Unmold on a hot platter. Garnish with parsley or watercress, and fill the center with sauce Robert.

Sauce Robert. One of the oldest French sauces, mentioned as early as the thirteenth century. It is appropriate for almost any kind of grilled, roast, or steamed meat, but especially for beef and pork.

In 2½ tablespoons of butter, simmer slowly, over a low flame, 1 large finely chopped onion until it is a very light gold, stirring frequently. Moisten with 1½ cups of dry white wine, and blend well, allowing the mixture to reduce one-third. Add 1 cup of rich brown sauce, stirring frequently, and allow to simmer for 15 minutes. (The original recipe calls for meat glaze, but this is too expensive to be used here.) Season to taste with salt and pepper,

1 generous pinch of granulated sugar, and 1 tablespoon of prepared mustard. Strain through a fine sieve into the center of the burger loaf ring. Serve at once. Do not allow the sauce to boil after adding the mustard.

*In 1630, Frenchmen believed that blue clothing aided digestion, and while this superstition reigned, nearly everyone wore at least one article that was blue in color.*

(181)

### BURGER SOUR-CREAM LOAF
*Serves 6 generously*

Mix well together ¼ cup of grated onion; ¼ cup of green pepper, ground; 2 cups of ground raw carrots; ¾ cup of heavy sour cream; 2 teaspoons of salt; ¼ generous teaspoon of black pepper; 1¾ pounds of lean raw ground beef; 3 strips of bacon, ground; 1 teaspoon of Worcestershire sauce; ¼ teaspoon of sage; ¼ teaspoon of thyme; ¼ teaspoon of clove; and 1 tablespoon of finely minced parsley. Pack lightly in a greased loaf pan, and crisscross the top. Bake for 1½ to 1¾ hours in a moderate oven (350 degrees F.). Dress on a hot platter. Garnish with watercress or parsley. Serve with egg cream sauce.

*Egg Cream Sauce.* Melt in a saucepan 2 tablespoons of butter, and blend in 2 tablespoons of flour. Do not allow to brown. When thoroughly blended and the mixture begins to bubble, stir in 2 cups of scalded milk, a little at a time, stirring briskly while pouring, to prevent lumping. Season to taste with salt and white pepper. Then beat in, off the fire, 2 fresh egg yolks, one at a time, beating well after each addition. Have ready 2 hard-cooked eggs. Shell, chop coarsely, and gently stir them into the sauce.

(182)

### BURGER WINE LOAF
*French method—serves 6 generously*

Mix thoroughly ¾ pound of lean raw ground beef chuck; ¾ pound of lean raw ground veal; ¾ pound of lean raw ground pork; 1 fair-sized clove of garlic, gently bruised; a bouquet garni composed of 1 large bay leaf, 6 sprigs of fresh parsley, 3 sprigs of green celery tops, and 1 sprig of thyme tied with white thread; 8 whole peppercorns, gently bruised; ½ teaspoon of sage; 2 whole cloves, bruised; and 3 leaflets of fresh fennel. Pour over this 1 cup of red wine, and mix well. Let stand overnight, covered with a buttered paper, in a cool place or in the refrigerator. Next day, beat the mixture well to incorporate the wine, which may float on the surface. Then fold in 2 egg whites, stiffly beaten.

Line a large ring mold with bacon strips, having the strips hanging on the side of the mold to about 2 inches, so as to fold them over the mixture after packing it lightly in the mold. Adjust the cover of the mold tightly. Place in a pan containing hot water, and bake in a very moderate oven (300 degrees F.) for 1½ hours. Remove the cover, and continue the baking for 15 to 20 minutes longer. Drain off the excess gravy floating on top of the mold. Invert the mold on a platter. Make a gravy from the drained mixture, thickening it if necessary, and pour it over the unmolded, luscious, tempting mixture. Garnish the center with a large bunch of watercress or, still better, with creamed mushrooms. Serve sizzling hot.

*In the eighteenth century, it was the custom for a Hungarian groom to drink wine from his bride's slipper at the wedding feast. He was supposed to drink one slipperful with each course.*

# INDEX

## A

Alder, 6
Allspice, 7
Anise, 7
Apple and burger patties, 14
Arnato, 7

## B

Bacon and burger grill, 15
Barbecued burger loaves, 22
Barbecued patties, 23
Basil, sweet, 12
Bay leaf, 7
Beef essence, 23, 24
Beef extract, 24
Borage, 7
Brown piquant sauce, 105
Brown snappy sauce, 29
Burger à la King, 50
Burger à la Ravenna, 60
Burger à la tartare, 77
Burger and banana grill, 36
Burger and carrot stew, 39
Burger and celery-root luncheon, 40
Burger and grated sweet potato casserole, 48
Burger and green peas casserole, 48
Burger and ham loaf, 97
Burger and mushroom au gratin, baked, 20
Burger and onion shortcake, 20
Burger and rice casserole dinner, 61
Burger and sauerkraut balls, 65
Burger applesauce casserole dinner, 31
Burger balls, baked, 18
  Finnish, 83
  Hungarian, 84
  juicy, 87
  Mexican, 87
  Polish, 35
  scalloped, 88

Swedish, 34
  with caper sauce, 38
  with creole sauce, 32
Burger balls à la Maryland, 34
Burger balls and kidney pie, 33
Burger balls and spaghetti meat sauce, 35
Burger balls fricassee, 33
Burger balls in spaghetti ring, 70
Burger balls in tomato gravy, 36
Burger balls vegetable dinner, baked, 16
Burger banana loaf, 95
Burger bay-leaf loaf, 95
Burger bean chili, 37
Burger bean dinner, 37–38
Burger, carrot, and banana loaf, 97
Burger casserole, Armenian, 15
Burger casserole, Brazilian, 26
Burger casserole au gratin, baked, 16
Burger casserole dinner, 39–40, 54
Burger chop suey, 41
Burger club plate ring, 42
Burger collops Yankee method, 42
Burger corn loaf, 96
Burger corn patties, 42
Burger croquettes, 43
Burger curried loaf, 96
Burger custard, baked, 18
Burger cutlets, 44
Burger Delmonico, 44
Burger dinner, 45
  bungalow, 31
  hunter's, 85
Burger double-crust pie, 55
Burger dumplings, 46
Burger essence, 24
Burger extract, 24
Burger fricadelle, à la romane, 47
  à la russe, 47
Burger gems with tomato sauce, baked, 12

Burger griddle cakes, 48
Burger grill en brochette, 49
Burger hodgepodge dinner, 49
Burger home style, baked, 20
Burger horseradish loaf, 98
Burger in corn custard squares, baked, 17
Burger in pastry jacket, 52
Burger in sour cream, 69
Burger liver loaf, 99
Burger loaf, Bohemian, 101
    cottage, 102
    country, 102, 103
    club, 103, 104
    farmer, 105
    Florida, 105
    home method, 106
    New England, 107
    steamed, 107
    with vegetables, 100
Burger luncheon, 45
Burger macaroni loaf dinner, 108
Burger mignon à la Stanley, 51
Burger mushroom-stuffed loaf, 109
Burger omelet à la tartare, 51
Burger on toast, creamed, 81
Burger oyster loaf, 110
Burger pasties, 52
Burger patties in potato jacket, 54
Burger patties shepherd's method, 54
Burger patty deep-dish pie, 53
Burger pickle-stuffed loaf, 110
Burger pie, Cuban, 81
    cottage, 81
    English, 82
    individual, 86
    in pumpkin crust, 21
Burger pinwheel loaf, 110, 111
Burger planked dinner, 56
Burger plate, Chinese, 80
Burger porcupines, 57
Burger pot roast dinner, 58
Burger potato sausage, 57
Burger ribbon loaf, 111
Burger ring loaf, 112
Burger ring mold, 62
Burger ragout à la creole, 59
Burger rarebit, 59
Burger rice cabbage rolls, 61

Burger roll, Flemish, 83
    stuffed, 89
Burger rolled-oats loaf, 113
Burger rolls luncheon, 62
Burger roly-poly, with olive sauce, 63
    with raisin sauce, 64
Burger salami loaf, 113
Burger sandwich grill, 65
Burger savory pudding, English, 82
Burger scrambled eggs, 66
Burger shortcake, 67
    Italian, 86
Burger soufflé, 68
Burger soup, 68
Burger sour-cream loaf, 114
Burger spaghetti casserole au gratin, 69
Burger spinach balls dinner, 70
Burger square, Swiss, 90
Burger steak, Florida, 46
    with soubise sauce, 71
    stuffed with eggs, 21
Burger stew, 71–72
Burger stew dinner, 30
Burger surprise, Haitian, 84
Burger tamale pie, 55, 76
Burger tartlets, individual, 86
Burger timbales, steamed, 89
Burger tomato cheese soufflé, 79
Burger tomato luncheon, 77
Burger tomato tart, 78
Burger turnovers, 78
Burger upside-down pie, 79
Burger vegetable pie, 56
Burger waffles, 80
Burger wine loaf, 114
Burger-cheese balls gourmet, baked, 17
Burger-cheese layer loaf, 98
Burger-onion layer loaf, 99
Burgers, braised, in tomato sauce, 24
Burgers, braised, in cabbage leaves, 25
    broiled, English style, 26
    on toast, 28
    southern method, 28
    with mushroom sauce, 27
    scraped, 88
Burnet, 7

D MASTERS, James T. Flexner. Four men emerged unexpectedly
l 18th century America to leadership in European art: Benjamin
ley, C. R. Peale, Gilbert Stuart. Brilliant coverage of lives and con-
ised, 1967 edition. 69 plates. 365pp. of text.

21806-6 Paperbound $3.00

S OF OUR WILDERNESS: AMERICAN PAINTING, THE COLONIAL
T. Flexner. Painters, and regional painting traditions from earliest
up to the emergence of Copley, West and Peale Sr., Foster, Gustavus
John Smibert and many anonymous painters in the primitive manner.
ntation, with 162 illustrations. xxii + 368pp.

22180-6 Paperbound $3.50

DISTANT SKIES: AMERICAN PAINTING, 1760-1835, James T. Flex-
generation of early American painters goes to Europe to learn and
Copley, Gilbert Stuart and others. Allston, Trumbull, Morse; also
nerican painters—primitives, derivatives, academics—who remained
illustrations. xiii + 306pp.        22179-2 Paperbound $3.50

HE RISE AND PROGRESS OF THE ARTS OF DESIGN IN THE UNITED
Dunlap. Much the richest mine of information on early American
s, architects, engravers, miniaturists, etc. The only source of in-
res of artists, the major primary source for many others. Unabridged
riginal 1834 edition, with new introduction by James T. Flexner,
strations. Edited by Rita Weiss. 6⅝ x 9⅝.
1695-0, 21696-9, 21697-7 Three volumes, Paperbound $13.50

NESE AND JAPANESE ART, Ernest F. Fenollosa. From primitive
20th century, thorough history, explanation of every important art
ncluding Japanese woodcuts; main stress on China and Japan, but
included. Still unexcelled for its detailed, rich coverage of cul-
aesthetic elements, diffusion studies, particularly of the historical
edition. 242 illustrations. lii + 439pp. of text.
20364-6, 20365-4 Two volumes, Paperbound $6.00

OF MAKING ENEMIES, James A. M. Whistler. Greatest wit of his
Wilde, Ruskin, Swinburne; strikes back at inane critics, exhibi-
m; aesthetics of impressionist revolution in most striking form.
lassic by great painter. Reproduction of edition designed by
tion by Alfred Werner. xxxvi + 334pp.

21875-9 Paperbound $3.00

**C**

Cabbage, burger-stuffed, 75
Capers, 7
Caraway seeds, 7
Cardamom seeds, 7
Casserole, Armenian, 15
  au gratin, 16
  Brazilian, 26
  burger, 39–40, 54
  burger and grated sweet potato, 48
  burger and green peas, 48
  burger and rice, 61
  burger applesauce, 31
  burger spaghetti, 69
Celery seeds, 8
Cheese-burger, broiled, 29
Chervil, 8
Chili, 8
Chili burgers, Arizona, 14
Chives, 8
Cinnamon, 8
Cloves, 8
Coriander, 8
Creamed burger on toast, 81
Cumin, 9
Curry powder, 9

**D**

Dill, 9
Dinner, bungalow, 31
  burger, 45
  burger and rice, 61
  burger applesauce, 31
  burger bean, 37–38
  burger casserole, 39–40, 54
  burger hodgepodge, 49
  burger pot roast, 58
  hunter's, 85
  planked, 56

**F**

Fennel, 9

**G**

Garlic, 9
Ginger, 9
Green peppers, burger-stuffed, 73
  cheese-stuffed, 62

**H**

Hamburg steak, original, 13
Herbs, use of, 5–6
Horehound, 9
Horseradish, 9
Hyssop, 9

**I**

Irish moss, 10

**J**

Juniper berries, 10

**L**

Lemon balm, 10
Licorice, 10
Luncheon, burger, 45
  burger and celery-root, 40
  burger rolls, 62
  burger tomato, 77

**M**

Mace, 10
Madeira sauce, 43
Marjoram, 10
Mint, 10
Moussaka, 15
Mustard, 10

**N**

Nutmeg, 10

**O**

Onion purée, 29
Onions, burger-stuffed, 73
  French fried, 28
Oregano, 10

**P**

Paprika, 11
Parsley, 11
Patties, apple and burger, 14
  barbecued, 23
  shepherd's, 54
Pepper, 11
Potatoes, Parisienne, 85
Poultry seasoning, 11

**R**

Raisin sauce, 64
Rosemary, 11

**S**

Saffron, 11
Sage, 11
Salisbury steaks, broiled, 29
Salt, 12
Sassafras, 12
Sauce, à la King, 51
    brown piquant, 105
    brown snappy, 29
    Madeira, 43
    raisin, 64
    Soubise, 71
    white, 90
Sauerkraut, 66
Sausage, burger potato, 57
    Rumanian, 88

Savory, 12
Sesame seeds, 12
Shallots, 12
Soubise sauce, 71
Spices, use of, 5–6
Spicy burgers, broiled, 30

**T**

Tabasco sauce, 12
Tansy, 12
Tarragon, 13
Thyme, 13
Tomatoes, burger stuffed, 74
Turmeric, 13

**W**

White sauce, 90
Woodruff, 13

A CATALOGUE O[
IN ALL F[

AMERICA'S O[
from provinci[
West, J. S. Co[
tributions. Re[

FIRST FLOWER[
PERIOD, James [
Colonial times [
Hesselius, Feke[
Engaging prese[

THE LIGHT OF [
ner. The great [
to teach: West, [
contemporary A[
in America. 10[

A HISTORY OF [
STATES, William [
painters, sculpto[
formation for sc[
reprint of rare o[
and 394 new illu[

EPOCHS OF CHI[
Chinese art to the[
period and form, [
Tibet, Korea also [
tural background, [
period. 2nd, 191[

THE GENTLE ART[
day deflates Oscar [
tions, art journalis[
Highly readable [
Whistler. Introdu[

VISUAL ILLUSIONS: THEIR CAUSES, CHARACTERISTICS, AND APPLICATIONS, Matthew Luckiesh. Thorough description and discussion of optical illusion, geometric and perspective, particularly; size and shape distortions, illusions of color, of motion; natural illusions; use of illusion in art and magic, industry, etc. Most useful today with op art, also for classical art. Scores of effects illustrated. Introduction by William H. Ittleson. 100 illustrations. xxi + 252pp.
21530-X Paperbound $2.00

A HANDBOOK OF ANATOMY FOR ART STUDENTS, Arthur Thomson. Thorough, virtually exhaustive coverage of skeletal structure, musculature, etc. Full text, supplemented by anatomical diagrams and drawings and by photographs of undraped figures. Unique in its comparison of male and female forms, pointing out differences of contour, texture, form. 211 figures, 40 drawings, 86 photographs. xx + 459pp. 5⅜ x 8⅜.
21163-0 Paperbound $3.50

150 MASTERPIECES OF DRAWING, Selected by Anthony Toney. Full page reproductions of drawings from the early 16th to the end of the 18th century, all beautifully reproduced: Rembrandt, Michelangelo, Dürer, Fragonard, Urs, Graf, Wouwerman, many others. First-rate browsing book, model book for artists. xviii + 150pp. 8⅜ x 11¼.
21032-4 Paperbound' $2.50

THE LATER WORK OF AUBREY BEARDSLEY, Aubrey Beardsley. Exotic, erotic, ironic masterpieces in full maturity: Comedy Ballet, Venus and Tannhauser, Pierrot, Lysistrata, Rape of the Lock, Savoy material, Ali Baba, Volpone, etc. This material revolutionized the art world, and is still powerful, fresh, brilliant. With *The Early Work,* all Beardsley's finest work. 174 plates, 2 in color. xiv + 176pp. 8⅛ x 11.
21817-1 Paperbound $3.00

DRAWINGS OF REMBRANDT, Rembrandt van Rijn. Complete reproduction of fabulously rare edition by Lippmann and Hofstede de Groot, completely reedited, updated, improved by Prof. Seymour Slive, Fogg Museum. Portraits, Biblical sketches, landscapes, Oriental types, nudes, episodes from classical mythology—All Rembrandt's fertile genius. Also selection of drawings by his pupils and followers. "Stunning volumes," *Saturday Review.* 550 illustrations. lxxviii + 552pp. 9⅛ x 12¼.
21485-0, 21486-9 Two volumes, Paperbound $10.00

THE DISASTERS OF WAR, Francisco Goya. One of the masterpieces of Western civilization—83 etchings that record Goya's shattering, bitter reaction to the Napoleonic war that swept through Spain after the insurrection of 1808 and to war in general. Reprint of the first edition, with three additional plates from Boston's Museum of Fine Arts. All plates facsimile size. Introduction by Philip Hofer, Fogg Museum. v + 97pp. 9⅜ x 8¼.
21872-4 Paperbound $2.00

GRAPHIC WORKS OF ODILON REDON. Largest collection of Redon's graphic works ever assembled: 172 lithographs, 28 etchings and engravings, 9 drawings. These include some of his most famous works. All the plates from *Odilon Redon: oeuvre graphique complet,* plus additional plates. New introduction and caption translations by Alfred Werner. 209 illustrations. xxvii + 209pp. 9⅛ x 12¼.
21966-8 Paperbound $4.00

DESIGN BY ACCIDENT; A BOOK OF "ACCIDENTAL EFFECTS" FOR ARTISTS AND DESIGNERS, James F. O'Brien. Create your own unique, striking, imaginative effects by "controlled accident" interaction of materials: paints and lacquers, oil and water based paints, splatter, crackling materials, shatter, similar items. Everything you do will be different; first book on this limitless art, so useful to both fine artist and commercial artist. Full instructions. 192 plates showing "accidents," 8 in color. viii + 215pp. 8⅜ x 11¼. 21942-9 Paperbound $3.50

THE BOOK OF SIGNS, Rudolf Koch. Famed German type designer draws 493 beautiful symbols: religious, mystical, alchemical, imperial, property marks, runes, etc. Remarkable fusion of traditional and modern. Good for suggestions of timelessness, smartness, modernity. Text. vi + 104pp. 6⅛ x 9¼. 20162-7 Paperbound $1.25

HISTORY OF INDIAN AND INDONESIAN ART, Ananda K. Coomaraswamy. An unabridged republication of one of the finest books by a great scholar in Eastern art. Rich in descriptive material, history, social backgrounds; Sunga reliefs, Rajput paintings, Gupta temples, Burmese frescoes, textiles, jewelry, sculpture, etc. 400 photos. viii + 423pp. 6⅜ x 9¾. 21436-2 Paperbound $5.00

PRIMITIVE ART, Franz Boas. America's foremost anthropologist surveys textiles, ceramics, woodcarving, basketry, metalwork, etc.; patterns, technology, creation of symbols, style origins. All areas of world, but very full on Northwest Coast Indians. More than 350 illustrations of baskets, boxes, totem poles, weapons, etc. 378 pp. 20025-6 Paperbound $3.00

THE GENTLEMAN AND CABINET MAKER'S DIRECTOR, Thomas Chippendale. Full reprint (third edition, 1762) of most influential furniture book of all time, by master cabinetmaker. 200 plates, illustrating chairs, sofas, mirrors, tables, cabinets, plus 24 photographs of surviving pieces. Biographical introduction by N. Bienenstock. vi + 249pp. 9⅞ x 12¾. 21601-2 Paperbound $4.00

AMERICAN ANTIQUE FURNITURE, Edgar G. Miller, Jr. The basic coverage of all American furniture before 1840. Individual chapters cover type of furniture—clocks, tables, sideboards, etc.—chronologically, with inexhaustible wealth of data. More than 2100 photographs, all identified, commented on. Essential to all early American collectors. Introduction by H. E. Keyes. vi + 1106pp. 7⅞ x 10¾. 21599-7, 21600-4 Two volumes, Paperbound $11.00

PENNSYLVANIA DUTCH AMERICAN FOLK ART, Henry J. Kauffman. 279 photos, 28 drawings of tulipware, Fraktur script, painted tinware, toys, flowered furniture, quilts, samplers, hex signs, house interiors, etc. Full descriptive text. Excellent for tourist, rewarding for designer, collector. Map. 146pp. 7⅞ x 10¾. 21205-X Paperbound $2.50

EARLY NEW ENGLAND GRAVESTONE RUBBINGS, Edmund V. Gillon, Jr. 43 photographs, 226 carefully reproduced rubbings show heavily symbolic, sometimes macabre early gravestones, up to early 19th century. Remarkable early American primitive art, occasionally strikingly beautiful; always powerful. Text. xxvi + 207pp. 8⅜ x 11¼. 21380-3 Paperbound $3.50

ALPHABETS AND ORNAMENTS, Ernst Lehner. Well-known pictorial source for decorative alphabets, script examples, cartouches, frames, decorative title pages, calligraphic initials, borders, similar material. 14th to 19th century, mostly European. Useful in almost any graphic arts designing, varied styles. 750 illustrations. 256pp. 7 x 10.    21905-4 Paperbound $4.00

PAINTING: A CREATIVE APPROACH, Norman Colquhoun. For the beginner simple guide provides an instructive approach to painting: major stumbling blocks for beginner; overcoming them, technical points; paints and pigments; oil painting; watercolor and other media and color. New section on "plastic" paints. Glossary. Formerly *Paint Your Own Pictures.* 221pp.    22000-1 Paperbound $1.75

THE ENJOYMENT AND USE OF COLOR, Walter Sargent. Explanation of the relations between colors themselves and between colors in nature and art, including hundreds of little-known facts about color values, intensities, effects of high and low illumination, complementary colors. Many practical hints for painters, references to great masters. 7 color plates, 29 illustrations. x + 274pp.
20944-X Paperbound $2.75

THE NOTEBOOKS OF LEONARDO DA VINCI, compiled and edited by Jean Paul Richter. 1566 extracts from original manuscripts reveal the full range of Leonardo's versatile genius: all his writings on painting, sculpture, architecture, anatomy, astronomy, geography, topography, physiology, mining, music, etc., in both Italian and English, with 186 plates of manuscript pages and more than 500 additional drawings. Includes studies for the Last Supper, the lost Sforza monument, and other works. Total of xlvii + 866pp. $7\frac{7}{8}$ x $10\frac{3}{4}$.
22572-0, 22573-9 Two volumes, Paperbound $10.00

MONTGOMERY WARD CATALOGUE OF 1895. Tea gowns, yards of flannel and pillow-case lace, stereoscopes, books of gospel hymns, the New Improved Singer Sewing Machine, side saddles, milk skimmers, straight-edged razors, high-button shoes, spittoons, and on and on . . . listing some 25,000 items, practically all illustrated. Essential to the shoppers of the 1890's, it is our truest record of the spirit of the period. Unaltered reprint of Issue No. 57, Spring and Summer 1895. Introduction by Boris Emmet. Innumerable illustrations. xiii + 624pp. $8\frac{1}{2}$ x $11\frac{5}{8}$.
22377-9 Paperbound $6.95

THE CRYSTAL PALACE EXHIBITION ILLUSTRATED CATALOGUE (LONDON, 1851). One of the wonders of the modern world—the Crystal Palace Exhibition in which all the nations of the civilized world exhibited their achievements in the arts and sciences—presented in an equally important illustrated catalogue. More than 1700 items pictured with accompanying text—ceramics, textiles, cast-iron work, carpets, pianos, sleds, razors, wall-papers, billiard tables, beehives, silverware and hundreds of other artifacts—represent the focal point of Victorian culture in the Western World. Probably the largest collection of Victorian decorative art ever assembled— indispensable for antiquarians and designers. Unabridged republication of the Art-Journal Catalogue of the Great Exhibition of 1851, with all terminal essays. New introduction by John Gloag, F.S.A. xxxiv + 426pp. 9 x 12.
22503-8 Paperbound $5.00

A HISTORY OF COSTUME, Carl Köhler. Definitive history, based on surviving pieces of clothing primarily, and paintings, statues, etc. secondarily. Highly readable text, supplemented by 594 illustrations of costumes of the ancient Mediterranean peoples, Greece and Rome, the Teutonic prehistoric period; costumes of the Middle Ages, Renaissance, Baroque, 18th and 19th centuries. Clear, measured patterns are provided for many clothing articles. Approach is practical throughout. Enlarged by Emma von Sichart. 464pp. 21030-8 Paperbound $3.50

ORIENTAL RUGS, ANTIQUE AND MODERN, Walter A. Hawley. A complete and authoritative treatise on the Oriental rug—where they are made, by whom and how, designs and symbols, characteristics in detail of the six major groups, how to distinguish them and how to buy them. Detailed technical data is provided on periods, weaves, warps, wefts, textures, sides, ends and knots, although no technical background is required for an understanding. 11 color plates, 80 halftones, 4 maps. vi + 320pp. 6⅛ x 9⅛. 22366-3 Paperbound $5.00

TEN BOOKS ON ARCHITECTURE, Vitruvius. By any standards the most important book on architecture ever written. Early Roman discussion of aesthetics of building, construction methods, orders, sites, and every other aspect of architecture has inspired, instructed architecture for about 2,000 years. Stands behind Palladio, Michelangelo, Bramante, Wren, countless others. Definitive Morris H. Morgan translation. 68 illustrations. xii + 331pp. 20645-9 Paperbound $3.00

THE FOUR BOOKS OF ARCHITECTURE, Andrea Palladio. Translated into every major Western European language in the two centuries following its publication in 1570, this has been one of the most influential books in the history of architecture. Complete reprint of the 1738 Isaac Ware edition. New introduction by Adolf Placzek, Columbia Univ. 216 plates. xxii + 110pp. of text. 9½ x 12¾.
21308-0 Clothbound $10.00

STICKS AND STONES: A STUDY OF AMERICAN ARCHITECTURE AND CIVILIZATION, Lewis Mumford.One of the great classics of American cultural history. American architecture from the medieval-inspired earliest forms to the early 20th century; evolution of structure and style, and reciprocal influences on environment. 21 photographic illustrations. 238pp. 20202-X Paperbound $2.00

THE AMERICAN BUILDER'S COMPANION, Asher Benjamin. The most widely used early 19th century architectural style and source book, for colonial up into Greek Revival periods. Extensive development of geometry of carpentering, construction of sashes, frames, doors, stairs; plans and elevations of domestic and other buildings. Hundreds of thousands of houses were built according to this book, now invaluable to historians, architects, restorers, etc. 1827 edition. 59 plates. 114pp. 7⅞ x 10¾.
22236-5 Paperbound $3.50

DUTCH HOUSES IN THE HUDSON VALLEY BEFORE 1776, Helen Wilkinson Reynolds. The standard survey of the Dutch colonial house and outbuildings, with constructional features, decoration, and local history associated with individual homesteads. Introduction by Franklin D. Roosevelt. Map. 150 illustrations. 469pp. 6⅝ x 9¼. 21469-9 Paperbound

## C

Cabbage, burger-stuffed, 75
Capers, 7
Caraway seeds, 7
Cardamom seeds, 7
Casserole, Armenian, 15
  au gratin, 16
  Brazilian, 26
  burger, 39–40, 54
  burger and grated sweet potato, 48
  burger and green peas, 48
  burger and rice, 61
  burger applesauce, 31
  burger spaghetti, 69
Celery seeds, 8
Cheese-burger, broiled, 29
Chervil, 8
Chili, 8
Chili burgers, Arizona, 14
Chives, 8
Cinnamon, 8
Cloves, 8
Coriander, 8
Creamed burger on toast, 81
Cumin, 9
Curry powder, 9

## D

Dill, 9
Dinner, bungalow, 31
  burger, 45
  burger and rice, 61
  burger applesauce, 31
  burger bean, 37–38
  burger casserole, 39–40, 54
  burger hodgepodge, 49
  burger pot roast, 58
  hunter's, 85
  planked, 56

## F

Fennel, 9

## G

Garlic, 9
Ginger, 9
Green peppers, burger-stuffed, 73
  cheese-stuffed, 62

## H

Hamburg steak, original, 13
Herbs, use of, 5–6
Horehound, 9
Horseradish, 9
Hyssop, 9

## I

Irish moss, 10

## J

Juniper berries, 10

## L

Lemon balm, 10
Licorice, 10
Luncheon, burger, 45
  burger and celery-root, 40
  burger rolls, 62
  burger tomato, 77

## M

Mace, 10
Madeira sauce, 43
Marjoram, 10
Mint, 10
Moussaka, 15
Mustard, 10

## N

Nutmeg, 10

## O

Onion purée, 29
Onions, burger-stuffed, 73
  French fried, 28
Oregano, 10

## P

Paprika, 11
Parsley, 11
Patties, apple and burger, 14
  barbecued, 23
  shepherd's, 54
Pepper, 11
Potatoes, Parisienne, 85
Poultry seasoning, 11

# Index

**R**

Raisin sauce, 64
Rosemary, 11

**S**

Saffron, 11
Sage, 11
Salisbury steaks, broiled, 29
Salt, 12
Sassafras, 12
Sauce, à la King, 51
   brown piquant, 105
   brown snappy, 29
   Madeira, 43
   raisin, 64
   Soubise, 71
   white, 90
Sauerkraut, 66
Sausage, burger potato, 57
   Rumanian, 88

Savory, 12
Sesame seeds, 12
Shallots, 12
Soubise sauce, 71
Spices, use of, 5–6
Spicy burgers, broiled, 30

**T**

Tabasco sauce, 12
Tansy, 12
Tarragon, 13
Thyme, 13
Tomatoes, burger stuffed, 74
Turmeric, 13

**W**

White sauce, 90
Woodruff, 13

# A CATALOGUE OF SELECTED DOVER BOOKS
## IN ALL FIELDS OF INTEREST

# A CATALOGUE OF SELECTED DOVER BOOKS
## IN ALL FIELDS OF INTEREST

AMERICA'S OLD MASTERS, James T. Flexner. Four men emerged unexpectedly from provincial 18th century America to leadership in European art: Benjamin West, J. S. Copley, C. R. Peale, Gilbert Stuart. Brilliant coverage of lives and contributions. Revised, 1967 edition. 69 plates. 365pp. of text.

21806-6 Paperbound $3.00

FIRST FLOWERS OF OUR WILDERNESS: AMERICAN PAINTING, THE COLONIAL PERIOD, James T. Flexner. Painters, and regional painting traditions from earliest Colonial times up to the emergence of Copley, West and Peale Sr., Foster, Gustavus Hesselius, Feke, John Smibert and many anonymous painters in the primitive manner. Engaging presentation, with 162 illustrations. xxii + 368pp.

22180-6 Paperbound $3.50

THE LIGHT OF DISTANT SKIES: AMERICAN PAINTING, 1760-1835, James T. Flexner. The great generation of early American painters goes to Europe to learn and to teach: West, Copley, Gilbert Stuart and others. Allston, Trumbull, Morse; also contemporary American painters—primitives, derivatives, academics—who remained in America. 102 illustrations. xiii + 306pp. 22179-2 Paperbound $3.50

A HISTORY OF THE RISE AND PROGRESS OF THE ARTS OF DESIGN IN THE UNITED STATES, William Dunlap. Much the richest mine of information on early American painters, sculptors, architects, engravers, miniaturists, etc. The only source of information for scores of artists, the major primary source for many others. Unabridged reprint of rare original 1834 edition, with new introduction by James T. Flexner, and 394 new illustrations. Edited by Rita Weiss. 6⅝ x 9⅝.

21695-0, 21696-9, 21697-7 Three volumes, Paperbound $13.50

EPOCHS OF CHINESE AND JAPANESE ART, Ernest F. Fenollosa. From primitive Chinese art to the 20th century, thorough history, explanation of every important art period and form, including Japanese woodcuts; main stress on China and Japan, but Tibet, Korea also included. Still unexcelled for its detailed, rich coverage of cultural background, aesthetic elements, diffusion studies, particularly of the historical period. 2nd, 1913 edition. 242 illustrations. lii + 439pp. of text.

20364-6, 20365-4 Two volumes, Paperbound $6.00

THE GENTLE ART OF MAKING ENEMIES, James A. M. Whistler. Greatest wit of his day deflates Oscar Wilde, Ruskin, Swinburne; strikes back at inane critics, exhibitions, art journalism; aesthetics of impressionist revolution in most striking form. Highly readable classic by great painter. Reproduction of edition designed by Whistler. Introduction by Alfred Werner. xxxvi + 334pp.

21875-9 Paperbound $3.00

VISUAL ILLUSIONS: THEIR CAUSES, CHARACTERISTICS, AND APPLICATIONS, Matthew Luckiesh. Thorough description and discussion of optical illusion, geometric and perspective, particularly; size and shape distortions, illusions of color, of motion; natural illusions; use of illusion in art and magic, industry, etc. Most useful today with op art, also for classical art. Scores of effects illustrated. Introduction by William H. Ittleson. 100 illustrations. xxi + 252pp.

21530-X Paperbound $2.00

A HANDBOOK OF ANATOMY FOR ART STUDENTS, Arthur Thomson. Thorough, virtually exhaustive coverage of skeletal structure, musculature, etc. Full text, supplemented by anatomical diagrams and drawings and by photographs of undraped figures. Unique in its comparison of male and female forms, pointing out differences of contour, texture, form. 211 figures, 40 drawings, 86 photographs. xx + 459pp. 5⅜ x 8⅜.

21163-0 Paperbound $3.50

150 MASTERPIECES OF DRAWING, Selected by Anthony Toney. Full page reproductions of drawings from the early 16th to the end of the 18th century, all beautifully reproduced: Rembrandt, Michelangelo, Dürer, Fragonard, Urs, Graf, Wouwerman, many others. First-rate browsing book, model book for artists. xviii + 150pp. 8⅜ x 11¼.

21032-4 Paperbound' $2.50

THE LATER WORK OF AUBREY BEARDSLEY, Aubrey Beardsley. Exotic, erotic, ironic masterpieces in full maturity: Comedy Ballet, Venus and Tannhauser, Pierrot, Lysistrata, Rape of the Lock, Savoy material, Ali Baba, Volpone, etc. This material revolutionized the art world, and is still powerful, fresh, brilliant. With *The Early Work,* all Beardsley's finest work. 174 plates, 2 in color. xiv + 176pp. 8⅛ x 11.

21817-1 Paperbound $3.00

DRAWINGS OF REMBRANDT, Rembrandt van Rijn. Complete reproduction of fabulously rare edition by Lippmann and Hofstede de Groot, completely reedited, updated, improved by Prof. Seymour Slive, Fogg Museum. Portraits, Biblical sketches, landscapes, Oriental types, nudes, episodes from classical mythology—All Rembrandt's fertile genius. Also selection of drawings by his pupils and followers. "Stunning volumes," *Saturday Review.* 550 illustrations. lxxviii + 552pp. 9⅛ x 12¼.

21485-0, 21486-9 Two volumes, Paperbound $10.00

THE DISASTERS OF WAR, Francisco Goya. One of the masterpieces of Western civilization—83 etchings that record Goya's shattering, bitter reaction to the Napoleonic war that swept through Spain after the insurrection of 1808 and to war in general. Reprint of the first edition, with three additional plates from Boston's Museum of Fine Arts. All plates facsimile size. Introduction by Philip Hofer, Fogg Museum. v + 97pp. 9⅜ x 8¼.

21872-4 Paperbound $2.00

GRAPHIC WORKS OF ODILON REDON. Largest collection of Redon's graphic works ever assembled: 172 lithographs, 28 etchings and engravings, 9 drawings. These include some of his most famous works. All the plates from *Odilon Redon: oeuvre graphique complet,* plus additional plates. New introduction and caption translations by Alfred Werner. 209 illustrations. xxvii + 209pp. 9⅛ x 12¼.

21966-8 Paperbound $4.00

DESIGN BY ACCIDENT; A BOOK OF "ACCIDENTAL EFFECTS" FOR ARTISTS AND DESIGNERS, James F. O'Brien. Create your own unique, striking, imaginative effects by "controlled accident" interaction of materials: paints and lacquers, oil and water based paints, splatter, crackling materials, shatter, similar items. Everything you do will be different; first book on this limitless art, so useful to both fine artist and commercial artist. Full instructions. 192 plates showing "accidents," 8 in color. viii + 215pp. 8⅜ x 11¼. 21942-9 Paperbound $3.50

THE BOOK OF SIGNS, Rudolf Koch. Famed German type designer draws 493 beautiful symbols: religious, mystical, alchemical, imperial, property marks, runes, etc. Remarkable fusion of traditional and modern. Good for suggestions of timelessness, smartness, modernity. Text. vi + 104pp. 6⅛ x 9¼. 20162-7 Paperbound $1.25

HISTORY OF INDIAN AND INDONESIAN ART, Ananda K. Coomaraswamy. An unabridged republication of one of the finest books by a great scholar in Eastern art. Rich in descriptive material, history, social backgrounds; Sunga reliefs, Rajput paintings, Gupta temples, Burmese frescoes, textiles, jewelry, sculpture, etc. 400 photos. viii + 423pp. 6⅜ x 9¾. 21436-2 Paperbound $5.00

PRIMITIVE ART, Franz Boas. America's foremost anthropologist surveys textiles, ceramics, woodcarving, basketry, metalwork, etc.; patterns, technology, creation of symbols, style origins. All areas of world, but very full on Northwest Coast Indians. More than 350 illustrations of baskets, boxes, totem poles, weapons, etc. 378 pp. 20025-6 Paperbound $3.00

THE GENTLEMAN AND CABINET MAKER'S DIRECTOR, Thomas Chippendale. Full reprint (third edition, 1762) of most influential furniture book of all time, by master cabinetmaker. 200 plates, illustrating chairs, sofas, mirrors, tables, cabinets, plus 24 photographs of surviving pieces. Biographical introduction by N. Bienenstock. vi + 249pp. 9⅞ x 12¾. 21601-2 Paperbound $4.00

AMERICAN ANTIQUE FURNITURE, Edgar G. Miller, Jr. The basic coverage of all American furniture before 1840. Individual chapters cover type of furniture— clocks, tables, sideboards, etc.—chronologically, with inexhaustible wealth of data. More than 2100 photographs, all identified, commented on. Essential to all early American collectors. Introduction by H. E. Keyes. vi + 1106pp. 7⅞ x 10¾. 21599-7, 21600-4 Two volumes, Paperbound $11.00

PENNSYLVANIA DUTCH AMERICAN FOLK ART, Henry J. Kauffman. 279 photos, 28 drawings of tulipware, Fraktur script, painted tinware, toys, flowered furniture, quilts, samplers, hex signs, house interiors, etc. Full descriptive text. Excellent for tourist, rewarding for designer, collector. Map. 146pp. 7⅞ x 10¾. 21205-X Paperbound $2.50

EARLY NEW ENGLAND GRAVESTONE RUBBINGS, Edmund V. Gillon, Jr. 43 photographs, 226 carefully reproduced rubbings show heavily symbolic, sometimes macabre early gravestones, up to early 19th century. Remarkable early American primitive art, occasionally strikingly beautiful; always powerful. Text. xxvi + 207pp. 8⅜ x 11¼. 21380-3 Paperbound $3.50

ALPHABETS AND ORNAMENTS, Ernst Lehner. Well-known pictorial source for decorative alphabets, script examples, cartouches, frames, decorative title pages, calligraphic initials, borders, similar material. 14th to 19th century, mostly European. Useful in almost any graphic arts designing, varied styles. 750 illustrations. 256pp. 7 x 10.                                          21905-4 Paperbound $4.00

PAINTING: A CREATIVE APPROACH, Norman Colquhoun. For the beginner simple guide provides an instructive approach to painting: major stumbling blocks for beginner; overcoming them, technical points; paints and pigments; oil painting; watercolor and other media and color. New section on "plastic" paints. Glossary. Formerly *Paint Your Own Pictures.* 221pp.          22000-1 Paperbound $1.75

THE ENJOYMENT AND USE OF COLOR, Walter Sargent. Explanation of the relations between colors themselves and between colors in nature and art, including hundreds of little-known facts about color values, intensities, effects of high and low illumination, complementary colors. Many practical hints for painters, references to great masters. 7 color plates, 29 illustrations. x + 274pp.
20944-X Paperbound $2.75

THE NOTEBOOKS OF LEONARDO DA VINCI, compiled and edited by Jean Paul Richter. 1566 extracts from original manuscripts reveal the full range of Leonardo's versatile genius: all his writings on painting, sculpture, architecture, anatomy, astronomy, geography, topography, physiology, mining, music, etc., in both Italian and English, with 186 plates of manuscript pages and more than 500 additional drawings. Includes studies for the Last Supper, the lost Sforza monument, and other works. Total of xlvii + 866pp. 7⅞ x 10¾.
22572-0, 22573-9 Two volumes, Paperbound $10.00

MONTGOMERY WARD CATALOGUE OF 1895. Tea gowns, yards of flannel and pillow-case lace, stereoscopes, books of gospel hymns, the New Improved Singer Sewing Machine, side saddles, milk skimmers, straight-edged razors, high-button shoes, spittoons, and on and on . . . listing some 25,000 items, practically all illustrated. Essential to the shoppers of the 1890's, it is our truest record of the spirit of the period. Unaltered reprint of Issue No. 57, Spring and Summer 1895. Introduction by Boris Emmet. Innumerable illustrations. xiii + 624pp. 8½ x 11⅝.
22377-9 Paperbound $6.95

THE CRYSTAL PALACE EXHIBITION ILLUSTRATED CATALOGUE (LONDON, 1851). One of the wonders of the modern world—the Crystal Palace Exhibition in which all the nations of the civilized world exhibited their achievements in the arts and sciences—presented in an equally important illustrated catalogue. More than 1700 items pictured with accompanying text—ceramics, textiles, cast-iron work, carpets, pianos, sleds, razors, wall-papers, billiard tables, beehives, silverware and hundreds of other artifacts—represent the focal point of Victorian culture in the Western World. Probably the largest collection of Victorian decorative art ever assembled— indispensable for antiquarians and designers. Unabridged republication of the Art-Journal Catalogue of the Great Exhibition of 1851, with all terminal essays. New introduction by John Gloag, F.S.A. xxxiv + 426pp. 9 x 12.
22503-8 Paperbound $5.00

A HISTORY OF COSTUME, Carl Köhler. Definitive history, based on surviving pieces of clothing primarily, and paintings, statues, etc. secondarily. Highly readable text, supplemented by 594 illustrations of costumes of the ancient Mediterranean peoples, Greece and Rome, the Teutonic prehistoric period; costumes of the Middle Ages, Renaissance, Baroque, 18th and 19th centuries. Clear, measured patterns are provided for many clothing articles. Approach is practical throughout. Enlarged by Emma von Sichart. 464pp. 21030-8 Paperbound $3.50.

ORIENTAL RUGS, ANTIQUE AND MODERN, Walter A. Hawley. A complete and authoritative treatise on the Oriental rug—where they are made, by whom and how, designs and symbols, characteristics in detail of the six major groups, how to distinguish them and how to buy them. Detailed technical data is provided on periods, weaves, warps, wefts, textures, sides, ends and knots, although no technical background is required for an understanding. 11 color plates, 80 halftones, 4 maps. vi + 320pp. 6⅛ x 9⅛. 22366-3 Paperbound $5.00

TEN BOOKS ON ARCHITECTURE, Vitruvius. By any standards the most important book on architecture ever written. Early Roman discussion of aesthetics of building, construction methods, orders, sites, and every other aspect of architecture has inspired, instructed architecture for about 2,000 years. Stands behind Palladio, Michelangelo, Bramante, Wren, countless others. Definitive Morris H. Morgan translation. 68 illustrations. xii + 331pp. 20645-9 Paperbound $3.00

THE FOUR BOOKS OF ARCHITECTURE, Andrea Palladio. Translated into every major Western European language in the two centuries following its publication in 1570, this has been one of the most influential books in the history of architecture. Complete reprint of the 1738 Isaac Ware edition. New introduction by Adolf Placzek, Columbia Univ. 216 plates. xxii + 110pp. of text. 9½ x 12¾. 21308-0 Clothbound $10.00

STICKS AND STONES: A STUDY OF AMERICAN ARCHITECTURE AND CIVILIZATION, Lewis Mumford.One of the great classics of American cultural history. American architecture from the medieval-inspired earliest forms to the early 20th century; evolution of structure and style, and reciprocal influences on environment. 21 photographic illustrations. 238pp. 20202-X Paperbound $2.00

THE AMERICAN BUILDER'S COMPANION, Asher Benjamin. The most widely used early 19th century architectural style and source book, for colonial up into Greek Revival periods. Extensive development of geometry of carpentering, construction of sashes, frames, doors, stairs; plans and elevations of domestic and other buildings. Hundreds of thousands of houses were built according to this book, now invaluable to historians, architects, restorers, etc. 1827 edition. 59 plates. 114pp. 7⅞ x 10¾. 22236-5 Paperbound $3.50

DUTCH HOUSES IN THE HUDSON VALLEY BEFORE 1776, Helen Wilkinson Reynolds. The standard survey of the Dutch colonial house and outbuildings, with constructional features, decoration, and local history associated with individual homesteads. Introduction by Franklin D. Roosevelt. Map. 150 illustrations. 469pp. 6⅝ x 9¼. 21469-9 Paperbound

THE ARCHITECTURE OF COUNTRY HOUSES, Andrew J. Downing. Together with Vaux's *Villas and Cottages* this is the basic book for Hudson River Gothic architecture of the middle Victorian period. Full, sound discussions of general aspects of housing, architecture, style, decoration, furnishing, together with scores of detailed house plans, illustrations of specific buildings, accompanied by full text. Perhaps the most influential single American architectural book. 1850 edition. Introduction by J. Stewart Johnson. 321 figures, 34 architectural designs. xvi + 560pp.
22003-6 Paperbound $4.00

LOST EXAMPLES OF COLONIAL ARCHITECTURE, John Mead Howells. Full-page photographs of buildings that have disappeared or been so altered as to be denatured, including many designed by major early American architects. 245 plates. xvii + 248pp. 7⅞ x 10¾. 21143-6 Paperbound $3.50

DOMESTIC ARCHITECTURE OF THE AMERICAN COLONIES AND OF THE EARLY REPUBLIC, Fiske Kimball. Foremost architect and restorer of Williamsburg and Monticello covers nearly 200 homes between 1620-1825. Architectural details, construction, style features, special fixtures, floor plans, etc. Generally considered finest work in its area. 219 illustrations of houses, doorways, windows, capital mantels. xx + 314pp. 7⅞ x 10¾. 21743-4 Paperbound $4.00

EARLY AMERICAN ROOMS: 1650-1858, edited by Russell Hawes Kettell. Tour of 12 rooms, each representative of a different era in American history and each furnished, decorated, designed and occupied in the style of the era. 72 plans and elevations, 8-page color section, etc., show fabrics, wall papers, arrangements, etc. Full descriptive text. xvii + 200pp. of text. 8⅜ x 11¼.
21633-0 Paperbound $5.00

THE FITZWILLIAM VIRGINAL BOOK, edited by J. Fuller Maitland and W. B. Squire. Full modern printing of famous early 17th-century ms. volume of 300 works by Morley, Byrd, Bull, Gibbons, etc. For piano or other modern keyboard instrument; easy to read format. xxxvi + 938pp. 8⅜ x 11.
21068-5, 21069-3 Two volumes, Paperbound $10.00

KEYBOARD MUSIC, Johann Sebastian Bach. Bach Gesellschaft edition. A rich selection of Bach's masterpieces for the harpsichord: the six English Suites, six French Suites, the six Partitas (Clavierübung part I), the Goldberg Variations (Clavierübung part IV), the fifteen Two-Part Inventions and the fifteen Three-Part Sinfonias. Clearly reproduced on large sheets with ample margins; eminently playable. vi + 312pp. 8⅛ x 11. 22360-4 Paperbound $5.00

THE MUSIC OF BACH: AN INTRODUCTION, Charles Sanford Terry. A fine, nontechnical introduction to Bach's music, both instrumental and vocal. Covers organ music, chamber music, passion music, other types. Analyzes themes, developments, innovations. x + 114pp. 21075-8 Paperbound $1.50

BEETHOVEN AND HIS NINE SYMPHONIES, Sir George Grove. Noted British musicologist provides best history, analysis, commentary on symphonies. Very thorough, rigorously accurate; necessary to both advanced student and amateur music lover. 436 musical passages. vii + 407 pp. 20334-4 Paperbound $2.75

JOHANN SEBASTIAN BACH, Philipp Spitta. One of the great classics of musicology, this definitive analysis of Bach's music (and life) has never been surpassed. Lucid, nontechnical analyses of hundreds of pieces (30 pages devoted to St. Matthew Passion, 26 to B Minor Mass). Also includes major analysis of 18th-century music. 450 musical examples. 40-page musical supplement. Total of xx + 1799pp.
(EUK) 22278-0, 22279-9 Two volumes, Clothbound $17.50

MOZART AND HIS PIANO CONCERTOS, Cuthbert Girdlestone. The only full-length study of an important area of Mozart's creativity. Provides detailed analyses of all 23 concertos, traces inspirational sources. 417 musical examples. Second edition. 509pp.
21271-8 Paperbound $3.50

THE PERFECT WAGNERITE: A COMMENTARY ON THE NIBLUNG'S RING, George Bernard Shaw. Brilliant and still relevant criticism in remarkable essays on Wagner's Ring cycle, Shaw's ideas on political and social ideology behind the plots, role of Leitmotifs, vocal requisites, etc. Prefaces. xxi + 136pp.
(USO) 21707-8 Paperbound $1.50

DON GIOVANNI, W. A. Mozart. Complete libretto, modern English translation; biographies of composer and librettist; accounts of early performances and critical reaction. Lavishly illustrated. All the material you need to understand and appreciate this great work. Dover Opera Guide and Libretto Series; translated and introduced by Ellen Bleiler. 92 illustrations. 209pp.
21134-7 Paperbound $2.00

BASIC ELECTRICITY, U. S. Bureau of Naval Personel. Originally a training course, best non-technical coverage of basic theory of electricity and its applications. Fundamental concepts, batteries, circuits, conductors and wiring techniques, AC and DC, inductance and capacitance, generators, motors, transformers, magnetic amplifiers, synchros, servomechanisms, etc. Also covers blue-prints, electrical diagrams, etc. Many questions, with answers. 349 illustrations. x + 448pp. 6½ x 9¼.
20973-3 Paperbound $3.50

REPRODUCTION OF SOUND, Edgar Villchur. Thorough coverage for laymen of high fidelity systems, reproducing systems in general, needles, amplifiers, preamps, loudspeakers, feedback, explaining physical background. "A rare talent for making technicalities vividly comprehensible," R. Darrell, *High Fidelity*. 69 figures. iv + 92pp.
21515-6 Paperbound $1.25

HEAR ME TALKIN' TO YA: THE STORY OF JAZZ AS TOLD BY THE MEN WHO MADE IT, Nat Shapiro and Nat Hentoff. Louis Armstrong, Fats Waller, Jo Jones, Clarence Williams, Billy Holiday, Duke Ellington, Jelly Roll Morton and dozens of other jazz greats tell how it was in Chicago's South Side, New Orleans, depression Harlem and the modern West Coast as jazz was born and grew. xvi + 429pp.
21726-4 Paperbound $3.00

FABLES OF AESOP, translated by Sir Roger L'Estrange. A reproduction of the very rare 1931 Paris edition; a selection of the most interesting fables, together with 50 imaginative drawings by Alexander Calder. v + 128pp. 6½x9¼.
21780-9 Paperbound $1.50

AGAINST THE GRAIN (A REBOURS), Joris K. Huysmans. Filled with weird images, evidences of a bizarre imagination, exotic experiments with hallucinatory drugs, rich tastes and smells and the diversions of its sybarite hero Duc Jean des Esseintes, this classic novel pushed 19th-century literary decadence to its limits. Full unabridged edition. Do not confuse this with abridged editions generally sold. Introduction by Havelock Ellis. xlix + 206pp. 22190-3 Paperbound $2.00

VARIORUM SHAKESPEARE: HAMLET. Edited by Horace H. Furness; a landmark of American scholarship. Exhaustive footnotes and appendices treat all doubtful words and phrases, as well as suggested critical emendations throughout the play's history. First volume contains editor's own text, collated with all Quartos and Folios. Second volume contains full first Quarto, translations of Shakespeare's sources (Belleforest, and Saxo Grammaticus), Der Bestrafte Brudermord, and many essays on critical and historical points of interest by major authorities of past and present. Includes details of staging and costuming over the years. By far the best edition available for serious students of Shakespeare. Total of xx + 905pp. 21004-9, 21005-7, 2 volumes, Paperbound $7.00

A LIFE OF WILLIAM SHAKESPEARE, Sir Sidney Lee. This is the standard life of Shakespeare, summarizing everything known about Shakespeare and his plays. Incredibly rich in material, broad in coverage, clear and judicious, it has served thousands as the best introduction to Shakespeare. 1931 edition. 9 plates. xxix + 792pp. (USO) 21967-4 Paperbound $3.75

MASTERS OF THE DRAMA, John Gassner. Most comprehensive history of the drama in print, covering every tradition from Greeks to modern Europe and America, including India, Far East, etc. Covers more than 800 dramatists, 2000 plays, with biographical material, plot summaries, theatre history, criticism, etc. "Best of its kind in English," *New Republic*. 77 illustrations. xxii + 890pp. 20100-7 Clothbound $8.50

THE EVOLUTION OF THE ENGLISH LANGUAGE, George McKnight. The growth of English, from the 14th century to the present. Unusual, non-technical account presents basic information in very interesting form: sound shifts, change in grammar and syntax, vocabulary growth, similar topics. Abundantly illustrated with quotations. Formerly *Modern English in the Making*. xii + 590pp. 21932-1 Paperbound $3.50

AN ETYMOLOGICAL DICTIONARY OF MODERN ENGLISH, Ernest Weekley. Fullest, richest work of its sort, by foremost British lexicographer. Detailed word histories, including many colloquial and archaic words; extensive quotations. Do not confuse this with the Concise Etymological Dictionary, which is much abridged. Total of xxvii + 830pp. 6½ x 9¼. 21873-2, 21874-0 Two volumes, Paperbound $7.90

FLATLAND: A ROMANCE OF MANY DIMENSIONS, E. A. Abbott. Classic of science-fiction explores ramifications of life in a two-dimensional world, and what happens when a three-dimensional being intrudes. Amusing reading, but also useful as introduction to thought about hyperspace. Introduction by Banesh Hoffmann. 16 illustrations. xx + 103pp. 20001-9 Paperbound $1.00

POEMS OF ANNE BRADSTREET, edited with an introduction by Robert Hutchinson. A new selection of poems by America's first poet and perhaps the first significant woman poet in the English language. 48 poems display her development in works of considerable variety—love poems, domestic poems, religious meditations, formal elegies, "quaternions," etc. Notes, bibliography. viii + 222pp.

22160-1 Paperbound $2.50

THREE GOTHIC NOVELS: THE CASTLE OF OTRANTO BY HORACE WALPOLE; VATHEK BY WILLIAM BECKFORD; THE VAMPYRE BY JOHN POLIDORI, WITH FRAGMENT OF A NOVEL BY LORD BYRON, edited by E. F. Bleiler. The first Gothic novel, by Walpole; the finest Oriental tale in English, by Beckford; powerful Romantic supernatural story in versions by Polidori and Byron. All extremely important in history of literature; all still exciting, packed with supernatural thrills, ghosts, haunted castles, magic, etc. xl + 291pp.

21232-7 Paperbound· $2.50

THE BEST TALES OF HOFFMANN, E. T. A. Hoffmann. 10 of Hoffmann's most important stories, in modern re-editings of standard translations: Nutcracker and the King of Mice, Signor Formica, Automata, The Sandman, Rath Krespel, The Golden Flowerpot, Master Martin the Cooper, The Mines of Falun, The King's Betrothed, A New Year's Eve Adventure. 7 illustrations by Hoffmann. Edited by E. F. Bleiler. xxxix + 419pp. 21793-0 Paperbound $3.00

GHOST AND HORROR STORIES OF AMBROSE BIERCE, Ambrose Bierce. 23 strikingly modern stories of the horrors latent in the human mind: The Eyes of the Panther, The Damned Thing, An Occurrence at Owl Creek Bridge, An Inhabitant of Carcosa, etc., plus the dream-essay, Visions of the Night. Edited by E. F. Bleiler. xxii + 199pp. 20767-6 Paperbound $1.50

BEST GHOST STORIES OF J. S. LEFANU, J. Sheridan LeFanu. Finest stories by Victorian master often considered greatest supernatural writer of all. Carmilla, Green Tea, The Haunted Baronet, The Familiar, and 12 others. Most never before available in the U. S. A. Edited by E. F. Bleiler. 8 illustrations from Victorian publications. xvii + 467pp. 20415-4 Paperbound $3.00

MATHEMATICAL FOUNDATIONS OF INFORMATION THEORY, A. I. Khinchin. Comprehensive introduction to work of Shannon, McMillan, Feinstein and Khinchin, placing these investigations on a rigorous mathematical basis. Covers entropy concept in probability theory, uniqueness theorem, Shannon's inequality, ergodic sources, the E property, martingale concept, noise, Feinstein's fundamental lemma, Shanon's first and second theorems. Translated by R. A. Silverman and M. D. Friedman. iii + 120pp. 60434-9 Paperbound $1.75

SEVEN SCIENCE FICTION NOVELS, H. G. Wells. The standard collection of the great novels. Complete, unabridged. *First Men in the Moon, Island of Dr. Moreau, War of the Worlds, Food of the Gods, Invisible Man, Time Machine, In the Days of the Comet.* Not only science fiction fans, but every educated person owes it to himself to read these novels. 1015pp. (USO) 20264-X Clothbound $6.00

LAST AND FIRST MEN AND STAR MAKER, TWO SCIENCE FICTION NOVELS, Olaf Stapledon. Greatest future histories in science fiction. In the first, human intelligence is the "hero," through strange paths of evolution, interplanetary invasions, incredible technologies, near extinctions and reemergences. Star Maker describes the quest of a band of star rovers for intelligence itself, through time and space: weird inhuman civilizations, crustacean minds, symbiotic worlds, etc. Complete, unabridged. v + 438pp. (USO) 21962-3 Paperbound $2.50

THREE PROPHETIC NOVELS, H. G. WELLS. Stages of a consistently planned future for mankind. *When the Sleeper Wakes,* and *A Story of the Days to Come,* anticipate *Brave New World* and *1984,* in the 21st Century; *The Time Machine,* only complete version in print, shows farther future and the end of mankind. All show Wells's greatest gifts as storyteller and novelist. Edited by E. F. Bleiler. x + 335pp. (USO) 20605-X Paperbound $2.50

THE DEVIL'S DICTIONARY, Ambrose Bierce. America's own Oscar Wilde— Ambrose Bierce—offers his barbed iconoclastic wisdom in over 1,000 definitions hailed by H. L. Mencken as "some of the most gorgeous witticisms in the English language." 145pp. 20487-1 Paperbound $1.25

MAX AND MORITZ, Wilhelm Busch. Great children's classic, father of comic strip, of two bad boys, Max and Moritz. Also Ker and Plunk (Plisch und Plumm), Cat and Mouse, Deceitful Henry, Ice-Peter, The Boy and the Pipe, and five other pieces. Original German, with English translation. Edited by H. Arthur Klein; translations by various hands and H. Arthur Klein. vi + 216pp. 20181-3 Paperbound $2.00

PIGS IS PIGS AND OTHER FAVORITES, Ellis Parker Butler. The title story is one of the best humor short stories, as Mike Flannery obfuscates biology and English. Also included, That Pup of Murchison's, The Great American Pie Company, and Perkins of Portland. 14 illustrations. v + 109pp. 21532-6 Paperbound $1.25

THE PETERKIN PAPERS, Lucretia P. Hale. It takes genius to be as stupidly mad as the Peterkins, as they decide to become wise, celebrate the "Fourth," keep a cow, and otherwise strain the resources of the Lady from Philadelphia. Basic book of American humor. 153 illustrations. 219pp. 20794-3 Paperbound $1.50

PERRAULT'S FAIRY TALES, translated by A. E. Johnson and S. R. Littlewood, with 34 full-page illustrations by Gustave Doré. All the original Perrault stories— Cinderella, Sleeping Beauty, Bluebeard, Little Red Riding Hood, Puss in Boots, Tom Thumb, etc.—with their witty verse morals and the magnificent illustrations of Doré. One of the five or six great books of European fairy tales. viii + 117pp. 8⅛ x 11. 22311-6 Paperbound $2.00

OLD HUNGARIAN FAIRY TALES, Baroness Orczy. Favorites translated and adapted by author of the *Scarlet Pimpernel.* Eight fairy tales include "The Suitors of Princess Fire-Fly," "The Twin Hunchbacks," "Mr. Cuttlefish's Love Story," and "The Enchanted Cat." This little volume of magic and adventure will captivate children as it has for generations. 90 drawings by Montagu Barstow. 96pp. 22293-4 Paperbound $1.95

THE RED FAIRY BOOK, Andrew Lang. Lang's color fairy books have long been children's favorites. This volume includes Rapunzel, Jack and the Bean-stalk and 35 other stories, familiar and unfamiliar. 4 plates, 93 illustrations x + 367pp.
21673-X Paperbound $2.50

THE BLUE FAIRY BOOK, Andrew Lang. Lang's tales come from all countries and all times. Here are 37 tales from Grimm, the Arabian Nights, Greek Mythology, and other fascinating sources. 8 plates, 130 illustrations. xi + 390pp.
21437-0 Paperbound $2.50

HOUSEHOLD STORIES BY THE BROTHERS GRIMM. Classic English-language edition of the well-known tales — Rumpelstiltskin, Snow White, Hansel and Gretel, The Twelve Brothers, Faithful John, Rapunzel, Tom Thumb (52 stories in all). Translated into simple, straightforward English by Lucy Crane. Ornamented with headpieces, vignettes, elaborate decorative initials and a dozen full-page illustrations by Walter Crane. x + 269pp.
21080-4 Paperbound $2.00

THE MERRY ADVENTURES OF ROBIN HOOD, Howard Pyle. The finest modern versions of the traditional ballads and tales about the great English outlaw. Howard Pyle's complete prose version, with every word, every illustration of the first edition. Do not confuse this facsimile of the original (1883) with modern editions that change text or illustrations. 23 plates plus many page decorations. xxii + 296pp.
22043-5 Paperbound $2.50

THE STORY OF KING ARTHUR AND HIS KNIGHTS, Howard Pyle. The finest children's version of the life of King Arthur; brilliantly retold by Pyle, with 48 of his most imaginative illustrations. xviii + 313pp. 6⅛ x 9¼.
21445-1 Paperbound $2.50

THE WONDERFUL WIZARD OF OZ, L. Frank Baum. America's finest children's book in facsimile of first edition with all Denslow illustrations in full color. The edition a child should have. Introduction by Martin Gardner. 23 color plates, scores of drawings. iv + 267pp.
20691-2 Paperbound $2.50

THE MARVELOUS LAND OF OZ, L. Frank Baum. The second Oz book, every bit as imaginative as the Wizard. The hero is a boy named Tip, but the Scarecrow and the Tin Woodman are back, as is the Oz magic. 16 color plates, 120 drawings by John R. Neill. 287pp.
20692-0 Paperbound $2.50

THE MAGICAL MONARCH OF MO, L. Frank Baum. Remarkable adventures in a land even stranger than Oz. The best of Baum's books not in the Oz series. 15 color plates and dozens of drawings by Frank Verbeck. xviii + 237pp.
21892-9 Paperbound $2.25

THE BAD CHILD'S BOOK OF BEASTS, MORE BEASTS FOR WORSE CHILDREN, A MORAL ALPHABET, Hilaire Belloc. Three complete humor classics in one volume. Be kind to the frog, and do not call him names . . . and 28 other whimsical animals. Familiar favorites and some not so well known. Illustrated by Basil Blackwell. 156pp.
(USO) 20749-8 Paperbound $1.50

EAST O' THE SUN AND WEST O' THE MOON, George W. Dasent. Considered the best of all translations of these Norwegian folk tales, this collection has been enjoyed by generations of children (and folklorists too). Includes True and Untrue, Why the Sea is Salt, East O' the Sun and West O' the Moon, Why the Bear is Stumpy-Tailed, Boots and the Troll, The Cock and the Hen, Rich Peter the Pedlar, and 52 more. The only edition with all 59 tales. 77 illustrations by Erik Werenskiold and Theodor Kittelsen. xv + 418pp. 22521-6 Paperbound $3.50

GOOPS AND HOW TO BE THEM, Gelett Burgess. Classic of tongue-in-cheek humor, masquerading as etiquette book. 87 verses, twice as many cartoons, show mischievous Goops as they demonstrate to children virtues of table manners, neatness, courtesy, etc. Favorite for generations. viii + 88pp. 6½ x 9¼. 22233-0 Paperbound $1.25

ALICE'S ADVENTURES UNDER GROUND, Lewis Carroll. The first version, quite different from the final Alice in Wonderland, printed out by Carroll himself with his own illustrations. Complete facsimile of the "million dollar" manuscript Carroll gave to Alice Liddell in 1864. Introduction by Martin Gardner. viii + 96pp. Title and dedication pages in color. 21482-6 Paperbound $1.25

THE BROWNIES, THEIR BOOK, Palmer Cox. Small as mice, cunning as foxes, exuberant and full of mischief, the Brownies go to the zoo, toy shop, seashore, circus, etc., in 24 verse adventures and 266 illustrations. Long a favorite, since their first appearance in St. Nicholas Magazine. xi + 144pp. 6⅝ x 9¼. 21265-3 Paperbound $1.75

SONGS OF CHILDHOOD, Walter De La Mare. Published (under the pseudonym Walter Ramal) when De La Mare was only 29, this charming collection has long been a favorite children's book. A facsimile of the first edition in paper, the 47 poems capture the simplicity of the nursery rhyme and the ballad, including such lyrics as I Met Eve, Tartary, The Silver Penny. vii + 106pp. (USO) 21972-0 Paperbound $1.25

THE COMPLETE NONSENSE OF EDWARD LEAR, Edward Lear. The finest 19th-century humorist-cartoonist in full: all nonsense limericks, zany alphabets, Owl and Pussycat, songs, nonsense botany, and more than 500 illustrations by Lear himself. Edited by Holbrook Jackson. xxix + 287pp. (USO) 20167-8 Paperbound $2.00

BILLY WHISKERS: THE AUTOBIOGRAPHY OF A GOAT, Frances Trego Montgomery. A favorite of children since the early 20th century, here are the escapades of that rambunctious, irresistible and mischievous goat—Billy Whiskers. Much in the spirit of Peck's Bad Boy, this is a book that children never tire of reading or hearing. All the original familiar illustrations by W. H. Fry are included: 6 color plates, 18 black and white drawings. 159pp. 22345-0 Paperbound $2.00

MOTHER GOOSE MELODIES. Faithful republication of the fabulously rare Munroe and Francis "copyright 1833" Boston edition—the most important Mother Goose collection, usually referred to as the "original." Familiar rhymes plus many rare ones, with wonderful old woodcut illustrations. Edited by E. F. Bleiler. 128pp. 4½ x 6⅜. 22577-1 Paperbound $1.00

TWO LITTLE SAVAGES; BEING THE ADVENTURES OF TWO BOYS WHO LIVED AS INDIANS AND WHAT THEY LEARNED, Ernest Thompson Seton. Great classic of nature and boyhood provides a vast range of woodlore in most palatable form, a genuinely entertaining story. Two farm boys build a teepee in woods and live in it for a month, working out Indian solutions to living problems, star lore, birds and animals, plants, etc. 293 illustrations. vii + 286pp.

20985-7 Paperbound $2.50

PETER PIPER'S PRACTICAL PRINCIPLES OF PLAIN & PERFECT PRONUNCIATION. Alliterative jingles and tongue-twisters of surprising charm, that made their first appearance in America about 1830. Republished in full with the spirited woodcut illustrations from this earliest American edition. 32pp. $4\frac{1}{2}$ x $6\frac{3}{8}$.

22560-7 Paperbound $1.00

SCIENCE EXPERIMENTS AND AMUSEMENTS FOR CHILDREN, Charles Vivian. 73 easy experiments, requiring only materials found at home or easily available, such as candles, coins, steel wool, etc.; illustrate basic phenomena like vacuum, simple chemical reaction, etc. All safe. Modern, well-planned. Formerly *Science Games for Children*. 102 photos, numerous drawings. 96pp. $6\frac{1}{8}$ x $9\frac{1}{4}$.

21856-2 Paperbound $1.25

AN INTRODUCTION TO CHESS MOVES AND TACTICS SIMPLY EXPLAINED, Leonard Barden. Informal intermediate introduction, quite strong in explaining reasons for moves. Covers basic material, tactics, important openings, traps, positional play in middle game, end game. Attempts to isolate patterns and recurrent configurations. Formerly *Chess*. 58 figures. 102pp. (USO) 21210-6 Paperbound $1.25

LASKER'S MANUAL OF CHESS, Dr. Emanuel Lasker. Lasker was not only one of the five great World Champions, he was also one of the ablest expositors, theorists, and analysts. In many ways, his Manual, permeated with his philosophy of battle, filled with keen insights, is one of the greatest works ever written on chess. Filled with analyzed games by the great players. A single-volume library that will profit almost any chess player, beginner or master. 308 diagrams. xli x 349pp.

20640-8 Paperbound $2.75

THE MASTER BOOK OF MATHEMATICAL RECREATIONS, Fred Schuh. In opinion of many the finest work ever prepared on mathematical puzzles, stunts, recreations; exhaustively thorough explanations of mathematics involved, analysis of effects, citation of puzzles and games. Mathematics involved is elementary. Translated by F. Göbel. 194 figures. xxiv + 430pp.

22134-2 Paperbound $3.50

MATHEMATICS, MAGIC AND MYSTERY, Martin Gardner. Puzzle editor for Scientific American explains mathematics behind various mystifying tricks: card tricks, stage "mind reading," coin and match tricks, counting out games, geometric dissections, etc. Probability sets, theory of numbers clearly explained. Also provides more than 400 tricks, guaranteed to work, that you can do. 135 illustrations. xii + 176pp.

20335-2 Paperbound $1.75

## CATALOGUE OF DOVER BOOKS

MATHEMATICAL PUZZLES FOR BEGINNERS AND ENTHUSIASTS, Geoffrey Mott-Smith. 189 puzzles from easy to difficult—involving arithmetic, logic, algebra, properties of digits, probability, etc.—for enjoyment and mental stimulus. Explanation of mathematical principles behind the puzzles. 135 illustrations. viii + 248pp.
20198-8 Paperbound $1.75

PAPER FOLDING FOR BEGINNERS, William D. Murray and Francis J. Rigney. Easiest book on the market, clearest instructions on making interesting, beautiful origami. Sail boats, cups, roosters, frogs that move legs, bonbon boxes, standing birds, etc. 40 projects; more than 275 diagrams and photographs. 94pp.
20713-7 Paperbound $1.00

TRICKS AND GAMES ON THE POOL TABLE, Fred Herrmann. 79 tricks and games—some solitaires, some for two or more players, some competitive games—to entertain you between formal games. Mystifying shots and throws, unusual caroms, tricks involving such props as cork, coins, a hat, etc. Formerly *Fun on the Pool Table*. 77 figures. 95pp.
21814-7 Paperbound $1.00

HAND SHADOWS TO BE THROWN UPON THE WALL: A SERIES OF NOVEL AND AMUSING FIGURES FORMED BY THE HAND, Henry Bursill. Delightful picturebook from great-grandfather's day shows how to make 18 different hand shadows: a bird that flies, duck that quacks, dog that wags his tail, camel, goose, deer, boy, turtle, etc. Only book of its sort. vi + 33pp. 6½ x 9¼. 21779-5 Paperbound $1.00

WHITTLING AND WOODCARVING, E. J. Tangerman. 18th printing of best book on market. "If you can cut a potato you can carve" toys and puzzles, chains, chessmen, caricatures, masks, frames, woodcut blocks, surface patterns, much more. Information on tools, woods, techniques. Also goes into serious wood sculpture from Middle Ages to present, East and West. 464 photos, figures. x + 293pp.
20965-2 Paperbound $2.00

HISTORY OF PHILOSOPHY, Julián Marias. Possibly the clearest, most easily followed, best planned, most useful one-volume history of philosophy on the market; neither skimpy nor overfull. Full details on system of every major philosopher and dozens of less important thinkers from pre-Socratics up to Existentialism and later. Strong on many European figures usually omitted. Has gone through dozens of editions in Europe. 1966 edition, translated by Stanley Appelbaum and Clarence Strowbridge. xviii + 505pp.
21739-6 Paperbound $3.50

YOGA: A SCIENTIFIC EVALUATION, Kovoor T. Behanan. Scientific but non-technical study of physiological results of yoga exercises; done under auspices of Yale U. Relations to Indian thought, to psychoanalysis, etc. 16 photos. xxiii + 270pp.
20505-3 Paperbound $2.50